STUDENT UNIT GUIDE

AQA | AS | UNIT 1

Sociology

Families and Households

Anne Brown

Series Editor: Joan Garrod

Philip Allan Updates, an imprint of Hodder Education, part of Hachette UK, Market Place, Deddington, Oxfordshire OX15 OSE

Orders

Bookpoint Ltd, 130 Milton Park, Abingdon, Oxfordshire, OX14 4SB
tel: 01235 827720
fax: 01235 400454
e-mail: uk.orders@bookpoint.co.uk
Lines are open 9.00 a.m.–5.00 p.m., Monday to Saturday, with a 24-hour message answering service. You can also order through the Philip Allan Updates website: www.philipallan.co.uk

© Philip Allan Updates 2008

ISBN 978-0-340-95805-6

First printed 2008
Impression number 5 4 3 2
2013 2012 2011 2010 2009

This guide has been written specifically to support students preparing for the AQA AS Sociology Unit 1 examination. The content has been neither approved nor endorsed by AQA and remains the sole responsibility of the author.

Typeset by Phoenix Photosetting, Chatham, Kent
Printed by MPG Books, Bodmin

Hachette UK's policy is to use papers that are natural, renewable and recyclable products and made from wood grown in sustainable forests. The logging and manufacturing processes are expected to conform to the environmental regulations of the country of origin.

P01234

Contents

Introduction

■ ■ ■

Content Guidance

■ ■ ■

Questions and Answers

■ ■ ■

Introduction

About this guide

This guide is about the **Families and Households** topic, which is part of Unit 1 of the AQA AS Sociology course. (Unit 1 also contains the topics of Culture and Identity, and Wealth, Poverty and Welfare.) When you have reached the end of the guide, you should have a clear sociological understanding of the nature of families and households in contemporary British society. You should also have knowledge and understanding of the main sociological perspectives on the family. The changes in family structure and the nature and extent of family diversity should be clear to you and you should understand the impact and effect of family arrangements on the individual. In addition, you should know how to prepare properly for the exam.

How to use the guide

When you start studying the family in class with your teacher, you can follow the relevant material in the **Content Guidance** section of this guide as your lessons progress. The information in this section provides a summary of all the areas you need to know for the exam.

Later on in your coverage of the topic, you can start to refer to the **Question and Answer** section. The unit test is marked out of 60 with the (a) section worth 2 marks, the (b) section worth 4 marks, the (c) section worth 6 marks and the (d) and (e) sections worth 24 marks each.

Begin by tackling all parts of the questions or choosing just one section to practise, such as the (d) or (e) sections. However, eventually you will need to answer a whole question in an hour, so the sooner you are comfortable with the structure of the questions, the better for your exam preparation.

When you attempt a whole question, follow this guidance:
(1) For each question you look at, read the **Items** carefully and make sure you understand them, noting any key words or concepts.
(2) Make sure that you are clear about what each question is asking you to do. This will go a long way to ensuring that you write a suitable answer.
(3) Read *all* sections of the question and make a note of the marks for each. Pay particular attention to the (d) and (e) questions: these account for 24 marks each. This point is crucially important as it should ensure that you do not make the **common mistake** of putting content in the wrong section because you have not read carefully and understood what each question is about.
(4) Time yourself and answer the question in 1 hour.
(5) When you have finished your self-test, refer to the examiner's comments and gauge whether your answer is a grade C or A. Note the ways in which marks can be gained and what you have to do to get into the higher bands.

The AS specification

There are a number of important definitions, concepts and key words that you will be expected to know and understand in the Families and Households topic. You will also be expected to have a good general historical knowledge of the changes in family and household structure and you will need to be able to discuss the current (contemporary) situation in relation to family diversity and change. As with all topics in sociology, there are several relevant research studies, and you will be expected to know some of these and use them in your answers. You will also need to be able to discuss their strengths and weaknesses.

Underpinning much of the topic is a comprehension of the key sociological perspectives or theories of the family, and a clear understanding of these will help to give you a better picture of what the sociological analysis of families and households is about. During your studies, you will learn that there are always a number of points of view on any topic, and your role as a student of sociology is to be able to evaluate the uses of each of them by pointing out and discussing their strengths and weaknesses.

The specification also contains some 'core themes' that must be incorporated into any topic you study. These are (a) socialisation, culture and identity and (b) social differentiation, power and stratification. Refer to the beginning of the **Content Guidance** section in this unit guide for an explanation of the meaning of these important concepts.

Examinable skills

Assessment objectives 1 and 2 (AO1 and AO2) are an integral part of the AS specification. The weighting of the two assessment objectives for AS Sociology is 40% of the total AS marks and 20% of the total for A-level.

Assessment objective 1 (AO1)

In AS Sociology Unit 1, **knowledge and understanding** carry 50% of the available marks. *Knowledge* of the subject or topic must be accurate to achieve marks, and you must also show that you have sufficient depth of knowledge. To demonstrate that you *understand* material, you must be able to select the right knowledge to answer a question and use it to show how it is relevant.

Knowledge and understanding must also be used sociologically to show that you can distinguish between explanations based on 'common-sense' knowledge and explanations arrived at through the study of sociological perspectives, methods and enquiry. AO1 involves knowledge and understanding of sociological theories, methods of enquiry, concepts and various forms of evidence. These fall into three broad areas, as detailed on the next page:

(a) **The nature of sociological thought** — you must understand the following concepts and theoretical issues:
- social order, social control
- social change
- conflict and consensus
- social structure and social action
- the role of values
- the relationship between sociology and contemporary social policy

(b) **Methods of sociological inquiry** — you must understand the range of methods and sources of data, the relationship between theory and methods and the ways sociologists deal with:
- the collection of primary and secondary data
- the analysis of quantitative and qualitative data
- factors influencing the design and conduct of sociological research
- practical, theoretical and ethical issues in sociological research

(c) **Themes** — you must understand how these themes apply to each topic and the global context:
- socialisation, culture and identity
- social differentiation, power and stratification

These themes are defined at the beginning of the Content Guidance section on page 12. The family is an important institution in relation to these themes in sociology as it plays a major role in the socialisation of children and adults, teaching cultural values and how we adopt an identity such as our gender roles. For example, we refer to the theme of social differentiation when we consider social class and ethnic factors in relation to family structures, and to roles, power and stratification when we look at areas such as gender roles and age patriarchy.

Assessment objective 2 (AO2)

AO2 involves **application, interpretation, analysis and evaluation**. These skills should be related to the AO1 skills outlined above and they carry 50% of the available marks. They fall into three broad areas:

(a) **Collection and recording of evidence** — you must demonstrate your ability to:
- analyse and evaluate the design of sociological investigations
- analyse and evaluate the method(s) used in studies to collect and record evidence

(b) **Interpretation and evaluation of evidence** — you must demonstrate your ability to:
- distinguish between facts, opinions and value judgements
- select and apply a range of relevant concepts and theories
- interpret quantitative and qualitative data
- identify and evaluate significant social trends shown in evidence
- evaluate theories, arguments and evidence

(c) **Presentation of evidence and argument** — you must demonstrate your ability to:
- organise evidence and communicate arguments in a coherent way
- demonstrate an awareness and understanding of theoretical debates in sociology
- use evidence to support arguments and conclusions

Quality of written communication

Make sure that your written work is *legible*. Spelling, punctuation and grammar must be accurate so that your meaning is made clear. Your writing style should be appropriate for AS and the information you present should be well organised. You *must* use specialist sociological vocabulary appropriately.

As you work through the topic, and particularly towards the end of it, your teacher will probably set you some practice exam questions to answer. Get into the habit of writing these under timed conditions so that when you sit the exam you can answer the question fully in the time you are given. Pay attention to your teacher's comments on your work and find out which skills you need to improve in order to achieve a better mark. Try to incorporate words that trigger evaluation skills at the beginning of sentences of the (d) and (e) sections, for example:
- 'However, another perspective argues...'
- 'A different argument put forward is...'
- 'Other evidence from research suggests...'
- 'On the other hand,...'
- 'An alternative view is...'
- 'A criticism of this is...'

Study skills and revision

Good study habits

Preparation for your examination should not be seen as a separate activity from actually learning the content of the topic in your lesson. Right from the first day you start your course, you should get yourself into good study habits. These next points should be thought of as additional to the work your teacher sets for you but they will also complement all the notes, handouts, questions, activities and tasks you carry out in your sociology lessons. If you follow these study skills guidelines, when you approach the time for your exam you will find that you have done much of the preparation necessary for success.
- Have a dedicated sociology folder with appropriate compartments for different topics, and have different sections within one topic area that are similar to the Content Guidance section of this unit guide. Put all materials straight into your folder when you get them. This way they will not get mislaid.
- Write the title of the topic on the front page of the appropriate section – for instance, 'Families and Households', followed by subheadings like 'Family and industrialisation', 'Different types of families', 'Divorce' and so on.

- Keep class notes and handouts in the *right order* in your folder. You can use the Content Guidance section of this unit guide to help organise your notes if you have not done this during the teaching of the topic.
- Keep your homework in a separate section at the back of your Families and Households section.
- Create a **glossary** for all definitions, key terms, concepts, new sociological words and a brief description of what each one means.
- Write a list of all the **sociological studies** you have learned. For each study, provide the title, author and date of the study, as well as an outline of the methods used and the main findings that add to our knowledge of the family. At least two criticisms should be included in your summary.
- At the end of each week, **review** your notes and make sure you have understood everything you have covered. Then write a brief paragraph explaining to yourself what you have learned that week.
- If you are issued with a textbook, there will be a relevant section to read every week. This will provide more information and detail to complement the Content Guidance section of this unit guide.

Revision

If you have been organised in making your folder, revision for the exam should be straightforward. All you will need to do is condense or summarise your notes into a more manageable form. Everyone has different ways of achieving this and sometimes it may take two or more attempts before you reduce the size of the notes to manageable proportions. The point here is that the process of condensing your notes helps you learn them. Here are some examples of different ways to revise that work for some students. If you were successful at GCSE, you may wish to use the same system you developed for your revision then.

- Get a large blank sheet of paper with the Families and Households title at the top of the page and write down everything you can remember off the top of your head. Go back to your notes and fill in the gaps. Remember this may take several attempts to get right. Use this as your revision sheet. Put it up on a wall (if allowed).
- On small filing cards break down the topic into areas that make sense to you and use these for reminders. Make sure you do not overcrowd each card with too much detail. You could use this method for revising studies, key concepts, key writers etc.
- Develop a colour-coded system that makes sense to you and reduce your notes to sections with one colour for headings, another for key concepts, another for studies and so on until everything is in order.
- Try to reduce your notes sufficiently to be manageable. You should aim to get all important content onto one side of A4 paper. This will take several attempts, so keep summarising until you have just got key words or phrases that tell you the main points.
- Draw spider diagrams, mind maps or brainstorm charts that have the topic title Families and Households in the middle of a page and then all the material you need to know radiating out from the centre. For a spider diagram, for example,

you use the legs of the spider to make links between different areas of the topic. One leg could be 'perspectives', another 'history', another could be 'childhood' and you keep doing this until you have covered the whole topic area.

- Get together with a small group of friends and test each other verbally on all areas of the topic, or allocate an area of the topic for one of you to revise and then explain to the group. Set yourselves short targets and give yourselves a small reward after you have finished a section.
- Use 'hot-seating' — this is where you give someone a role to play or an aspect of the topic to learn, and he or she then sits in the hot-seat and you can ask him or her questions about his or her 'subject'. Asking questions can often help you learn more than answering questions, and this is something you can do for yourself to test your own knowledge.

Remember: there is no 'right' or 'wrong' way to learn something. You need to find a way that works *for you*. Keep in mind that it is more productive to work in short blocks of time and often rather than one long block of time. When you reach a target or achieve a goal, give yourself a little reward.

The unit test

The paper

Families and Households is the second topic of Unit 1 of the AS specification. The unit also contains the topics of Culture and Identity, and Wealth, Poverty and Welfare. The question paper will contain questions on all three topics. Ensure that you answer only the Families and Households question. You will have **1 hour** to answer the question, which carries a total of **60 marks**. The unit as a whole is worth 40% of the total marks available for AS Sociology and 20% of the total marks for A-level.

Question structure

The question usually involves reading or studying two Items. The instructions on the paper will state 'Read Items 2A and 2B below and answer parts (a) to (e) that follow'.

Follow the guidance to the letter and do not start writing before you have read the Items and all the questions.

Five questions labelled (a) to (e) follow the Items. The amount you write for each answer should relate to the marks you can achieve.

- The **(a) question** carries **2 marks** so you should only need to write a sentence or two.
- The **(b) question** carries **4 marks** and usually asks for two ways in which something has happened in family life, or two examples of something. To gain the full 4 marks, you must provide two such descriptions or examples. Make sure you give two distinct sections for the examiner to see clearly that you have answered

the question correctly. Two sentences for each 'way' or example should gain full marks if written clearly.

- The **(c) question** carries **6 marks**. This question usually asks for three reasons for something — for example, a change that has taken place in an aspect of family life. To gain the full 6 marks you will need to provide three distinct reasons and lay out your answer clearly in three parts that give the first reason, the second reason and the third reason without any duplication. A common mistake is to overlap or repeat answers, so make sure yours are three quite separate reasons.
- The **(d) question** carries 24 marks. Treat this as an essay-type answer. The key command word at the beginning of the sentence — such as 'examine' — should trigger in your mind what you have to do. The answer to section (d) will be a substantial piece of work that should be written in a way that shows your conceptual knowledge and understanding of the area and sociological material connected to it. You should include studies and key writers where relevant and elaborate fully on the points you are making. The material you use should be well organised, accurate, relevant to the question and coherent. You should analyse and evaluate material as appropriate. Your answer should contain an introduction and a conclusion.
- The **(e) section** carries **24 marks** and usually asks you to assess something. You will be asked to use evidence from the Items and elsewhere. To do this try to incorporate phrases similar to the following ones as a means of integrating the material from the Item(s) into your answer — remember these are only suggestions:
  - 'The view referred to in Item A is that...'
  - 'Item B reflects a feminist perspective that has been criticised...'
  - 'The examples given in Item B...'
  - 'Item B shows evidence of...'
  - 'A particular strength of the view expressed in Item B is...'
  - 'Another way to look at the evidence in the Items is...'

  Once again, this is an essay-type answer where you should put together a coherent argument that answers the question directly. You will be marked on your ability to show analytical and evaluation skills. You must show a clear rationale for your answer and the material you use should be relevant to the question, well organised, thorough, accurate and sufficiently detailed.

Command words

You should have learned the meaning of words like 'assess', 'discuss' and 'evaluate', which will appear in the (d) and (e) sections of the question. Generally, they mean to consider the evidence, weigh up arguments for and against an issue, approach or view, provide critical judgements and draw a conclusion.

Content
Guidance

This section is intended to cover the major areas or topics in the **Families and Households** unit, together with some studies. Remember that these are offered for guidance only — the coverage is neither exhaustive nor exclusive. The information provided is in a summarised form and you should use your class notes, textbook and the magazine *Sociology Review* (if available) to make sure you have covered the topic in sufficient detail and depth. There will be references to key studies that sociologists have carried out on Families and Households, but your teacher and your textbook will provide further examples.

The AS specification for Families and Households is divided into the following sections, and this section of the unit guide will broadly follow its contents:

- the relationship of the family to the social structure and social change, with particular reference to the economy and to state policies
- changes in patterns of marriage, cohabitation, separation, divorce, child-bearing and the life course; the diversity of contemporary family and household structures
- the nature and extent of changes within the family, with reference to gender roles, domestic labour and power relationships
- the nature of childhood and changes in the status of children in the family and society
- demographic trends in the UK since 1900; reasons for changes in birth rates, death rates and family size

The core themes explored are:

- **Socialisation** — the means by which we are taught and learn the norms, values and expected ways to behave in society, starting in childhood and continuing throughout our lives.
- **Culture** — the way of life, belief systems, values, norms, habits and attitudes of a group of people.
- **Identity** — the concepts we use to define ourselves as individuals and members of groups, such as gender, age or ethnicity.
- **Social differentiation** — the divisions and differences that exist between individuals and groups of people.
- **Power** — the ability or inability we have to affect decisions made about our lives.
- **Stratification** — the hierarchy of power that exists on numerous levels or layers in society. Social stratification is usually defined as based on social class but can also be related to other areas such as ethnicity, gender, age, jobs, skills, educational qualifications etc.

Module content

The following section is a brief outline of what the Families and Households topic is all about. It contains all the information that you should know before your exam.

The relationship of the family to the social structure and social change, with particular reference to the economy and to state policies.

- There are different views of the relationship of the family to the society (social structure). These are the sociological theories or perspectives about the family and society. The main ones you need to know are the (i) functionalist, (ii) Marxist, (iii) interpretivist, (iv) feminist, (v) New Right and (vi) postmodern views. You should know some of the similarities and differences of the perspectives, as well as be able to discuss the strengths and weaknesses of each one.
- The links between the family and the economy are seen differently by the different perspectives and you should be able to apply your knowledge of the perspectives to an understanding of the relationship between the role of the family and the economic structure of society and the world of work. Industrialisation and urbanisation are processes that have affected the role and structure of the family, as is the changing nature of work and the workforce.
- The role and structure of the family have been influenced and changed by social policies that governments have introduced. You should know the major policies in outline, and what effects they have had on family life and household structure. You should be aware that changes in the family can influence government views, which can lead to new social policies.

Changes in patterns of marriage, cohabitation, separation, divorce, child-bearing and the life course, and the diversity of contemporary family and household structures.

- The form that families and households have taken has altered over time. Family size varies, relationships between members and patterns of family living change, and the way children are brought up has changed. Over a lifetime there are changes in how we live and what kinds of households we live in.
- The evidence about the relationship between industrialisation, urbanisation and changing family structure must be understood in terms of the characteristics of the family before and after these processes took place. Other shifts are related to the changing nature of work and to the effects of the UK being a multi-cultural society.

The nature and extent of changes within the family, with particular reference to gender roles, domestic labour and power relationships.

- The nature (what kind) and extent (how much) of change in the 'domestic division of labour' is debated. Who does the housework and/or childcare? What has changed? Women now go out to work but also do the majority of the domestic work in the house. Is the family still a patriarchal institution?

- Men and women both earn money and women now have more legal rights. Has this changed the power relationships between men and women?
- The role of children and the nature of child-rearing has changed, so have the relationships between adults and children.

The nature of childhood, and changes in the status of children in the family and society.

- The 'nature of childhood' means what childhood is like — what it means to be a child in a family and in society.
- Changes in childhood refer to the changing role of childhood, for example in the past children would have worked to earn money from quite a young age, whereas today in Western societies children are required by law to go to school. These changes have affected the way we perceive children and how we expect them to behave. There are many cross-cultural variations in the status of children.
- The role of children as part of a family and the ways in which children are expected to participate in society have undergone many changes over the last 100 years. Indeed, the way we perceive childhood is ever-changing and this is a feature of family life.
- It is estimated that one in four children is now brought up by a single parent at some stage during childhood.

Demographic trends in the UK since 1900 and reasons for changes in birth rates, death rates and family size.

- Demography is the study of population statistics and trends that can be measured. Records of many aspects of family life have been kept systematically by the government for many years.
- The reasons why fertility rates, birth rates, death rates and family size have changed will be covered in relation to other aspects of societal change, such as the changing role of women and men, developments in reproductive technology, changes in work patterns and affluence.

Each of the following subsections relates to the content headings for the unit in the specification.

Relationship of the family to social structure and social change

Key ideas

You should know the meaning of the terms 'families' and 'households'. Make sure you also understand the following key terms:

- **Social structure** is a relatively stable social formation that has its own role beyond that of the individual. A society is an example of social structure. The family and the education system are social structures. Language is a social structure.

- **Social change** occurs when an aspect of society moves into a different state of being. The family changed during the processes of industrialisation and urbanisation. An example of a social change today is that families are generally smaller than in the past.
- **Economy** usually refers to the ways in which production is organised, who has control over material resources and how money is controlled.

The 'different views' already referred to are the sociological theories or perspectives that provide you with an overview of ways to understand the role of the family in society and how the family has changed over time.

There is still debate about whether the family changed from an extended to a nuclear structure with the advent of the Industrial Revolution. There is evidence for and against. Each perspective has its own ideas about the changes resulting from industrialisation and urbanisation. The work of Laslett and Anderson, for instance, indicates that the process has not been straightforward — there is evidence that extended families exist in industrial society and that nuclear families existed in pre-industrial society. In addition, people in families of South Asian, Pakistani, Cypriot and Bangladeshi heritage have maintained close relationships with wider kin even though many were born and are living in an industrial society. It is also important to note that working-class families are more likely to maintain close contact with extended kin than middle-class families.

Functionalist perspective

Based largely on American sociology of the 1940s and 1950s, the functionalist perspective assumes that the family is essential to the survival of society:
- The family is a universal institution that exists in one form or another in all societies.
- The family performs basic functions or serves purposes for the individual and society. These functions are:
  - an economic function — providing money, food, shelter for members of the family
  - a sexual/reproductive function — setting norms governing 'appropriate' sexual relationships to produce the next generation
  - a socialisation function — teaching children the language, norms and values of society
  - the stabilisation of adult personalities — women as mothers/carers; fathers as breadwinners/providers
- The dominant structure of the family best suits the needs of the economy at the time. Thus, the move from a rural, agricultural society to an urban, industrial economy brought about changes from a largely extended, family-based unit of production to a nuclear unit of consumption, where paid work takes place outside the home. This means that nuclear families need to be geographically mobile and not reliant on wider kin so that members can easily move to new centres of production to find work.

New Right perspectives

New Right perspectives are related closely to functionalism but with added political rather than sociological dimensions related to the Conservative Party in the UK and the Republican Party in the USA. Based on the political period of the late 1970s to the late 1990s when the Conservative Party was in power in the UK, New Right views:

- promoted the nuclear family (two heterosexual [different sex] married partners and their children) as the 'best' form of the family
- supported traditional roles for men and women in the family — women as wives/mothers, men as providers/fathers
- claimed that the decline of 'family values' led to social problems such as crime, poor educational achievement and aspirations, anti-social behaviour, increases in single-parent families and the creation of an underclass

New Right and functionalist views see the family as a support for the economy by providing children who are socialised to work hard and strive for a good job. In the past the extended family would have supported the agricultural rural-based economy; now the nuclear family supports the needs of an industrial, urban-based economy. The nuclear family is best suited to geographical mobility whereby small family units can move around to the centres of production. Hence, the decline of the extended family after the industrial revolution was a natural change.

Key concepts

extended family; nuclear family; functions of the family; primary socialisation; needs of society; universal family; traditional family values; underclass; industrialisation; urbanisation; geographical mobility

Key writers

Durkheim, Fletcher, Murdock, Murray, Talcott Parsons

Evaluation

+ Functionalists point to the positive experiences of nuclear family life for some people.
+ Functionalists see society as whole and the family as one aspect that helps to stabilise the workings of society by, for example, bringing up children and socialising them appropriately.
− There is evidence that undermines the idea of the universal nuclear family, e.g. Nayar.
− The negative and 'darker' sides to family life, such as divorce, domestic violence and child abuse, are neglected.
− The diversity of family life is not recognised, and the nuclear family is promoted as the norm in industrial society.
− The theory cannot account for the changes that have taken place in families and the increases in single-person households.

- The theory takes a traditional view of family roles, whereas now most women take part in paid employment outside the home.
- There is some dispute about the move from extended to nuclear families during industrialisation, as there is evidence that nuclear families existed in pre-industrial society and that extended families exist in industrial society, e.g. families in the East End of London, Asian families and those of Cypriot heritage.

Marxist perspectives

Marxist perspectives on the family are based largely on the writings of Engels, a close collaborator of Marx, who tried to link archaeological evidence to the notion of a 'primitive communism' that may have existed in the ancient world where families were communal. Engels argued that the modern nuclear family emerged because of the rise in the private ownership of property based on social class relations between the bourgeoisie and the proletariat. This meant that the only way to trace ancestry was through monogamous marriage and the male line.

- For both Marx and Engels, the economy is the dominant feature of capitalist society. Therefore, the family must be closely connected to the needs of the economy. Some writers have called this 'economic determinism'. First, the family provides the next generation of workers to enter production, so the family is a source of 'labour power'. Second, through socialisation the family instils capitalist ideology into the values and attitudes of its members. We give our active consent to the domination of the ruling class. The role of the family is similar to that of the mass media, religion and education in maintaining and justifying the inequality that exists in a capitalist society.
- Women provide domestic labour free for the capitalists in that they care for other family members for no payment. Women are also a reserve army of labour and can be drawn into the labour market when needed. Women provide emotional support to families, alleviating the strains and frustration of work under capitalism.
- Men are the breadwinners and have most of the authority in the family. A man's need to provide financial support for the family acts to control him by making sure that his paid employment is necessary for family survival and his ability to withdraw labour or go on strike is minimised.
- There is conflict in the family, which reflects the wider conflict between social classes in the wider society.
- The family in capitalist society oppresses women particularly.
- The family is a unit of consumption.

Key concepts

social class; economic determinism; bourgeoisie; proletariat; capitalism; ideology; domestic labour; reserve army of labour

Key writers

Engels, Gramsci, Marx, Zaretsky

Evaluation

+ Marxists theorise the family from a capitalist perspective and can therefore explain conflict in the family.
+ Marxists adopt a critical view of the role of the family in society.
+ Marxists link ideology to the role of the family.
− Marxists sees the nature and role of the family as directly connected to the needs of the economy — economic determinism.
− Marxists focus on the negative and exploitative aspects of the family.
− Marxists do not acknowledge the positive benefits of family life for individuals and society.

Interpretivist perspective

The approach adopted by interpretivist sociologists or action theorists is to ask what the family is really like for its members and what it represents for them. The roles, relationships and meaning individuals give to their family lives are at the heart of this perspective. Interpretivists concentrate on individual action and the nature of interpersonal power relationships in the family. Therefore, research often adopts a qualitative methodology, using in-depth interviews and case studies in an attempt to understand how people construct their versions of reality and give meaning to their family lives.

Studies conducted by interpretivist sociologists tend to focus on how conjugal roles in marriage are constructed and how husbands and wives give meaning to the roles that they are playing. The processes by which couples come to understand and negotiate the reality of their married life have been a key aspect of interpretivist understanding of marriage and the family. Interpretivist theorists have tried to identify types of marriage as well as how early-marriage roles and relationships may change over time and with the addition of children and the variation of working patterns. For example, Clarke points to the importance of active processes that renegotiate marriage patterns in order to stabilise marriage and create shared meanings in the family.

Ideas about the meaning and importance of romantic love have been combined with some feminist research which shows that only recently has this notion become a central plank of marriage. The ideology of romance is part of the socialisation of young girls and women and leads to high expectations of marriage that become one of the main goals to achieve in life.

Key concepts

interpretive meaning; interpretive understanding; negotiation; roles; social construction of reality; action; actors; verstehen; romantic love; 'new action theory'

Key writers

Berger and Kellner, Clarke, Mansfield and Collard, McRobbie

Evaluation

+ The interpretivist perspective allows us to see the hidden meanings that individuals have of their roles and relationships in the family.
+ It contrasts with the structural approaches of the functionalist, Marxist and some feminist perspectives.
+ It takes us beyond the common-sense notions of what the family is like and helps us understand the actual meaning people give to their family life.
− It concentrates on the individual meanings and interpretations and neglects wider structures in society which may affect the way families operate and are organised.
− It has difficulty in explaining and understanding the broader effects of social policies on the family because structure is separated from action.

Feminist perspectives

You should be aware that there are a variety of feminist views on the family. You should know some of the differences between them — for example, Marxist feminist, radical feminist and liberal feminist.

Marxist feminist

- The nuclear family serves the needs of capitalism and controls the roles of its members — men primarily go out to work, women are socialised to be mothers and carers.
- Women play a secondary role to men and are exploited by them. Women are exploited by capitalism and treated as a reserve army of labour.

Radical feminist

- The main oppression of women is by men, both inside and outside the family.
- What seems to be personal choice about roles in marriage and the family is in fact a political system of ideological control by and for the benefit of men.
- The family is part of a wider patriarchal system of oppression in society. Women and men are seen as 'sex-classes', whose roles are socially constructed.

Liberal feminist

- Campaigning feminists who believe that existing society can bring about equal rights for women both in society and in family life.
- The second-class status of women can be changed through the reform of the laws that govern rights and responsibilities in society such as the Equal Pay Act 1975 and the Sex Discrimination Act 1975.

Other feminist views include: black feminist, socialist feminist, post-feminist, dual-systems feminism (class and gender interplay) and triple-systems feminism (interplay between class, gender and ethnicity).

Key concepts

patriarchy; matriarchy; oppression; women's rights; socially constructed roles; socialisation; ideological control

Key writers

Amos and Parmar, Barrett, Benston, Delphy, Firestone, Greer, Leonard, Oakley, Walby

Evaluation

+ Feminist perspectives changed the traditional focus of the sociology of the family, which accepted the nature of family roles as 'natural', where women are mothers and men are breadwinners.
+ They focus on women's role and try to redress the historical balance of sociology, which focused on men or portrayed women as one-dimensional.
+ Some feminists have adopted an approach to the family that can account for a range of different experiences women may have of family life.
+ They are useful to sociology generally because of their critical and radical approach, but particularly because of the way in which they have challenged the simplistic functionalist approach to the family.
− They fail to take account of variation in family structures and roles.
− There is the assumption that all women are exploited and oppressed, and a failure to recognise that family is experienced differently by different women.
− They neglect the positive aspects of family life, particularly for women.

Postmodern perspective

- No one type of family should be viewed as more desirable or acceptable than others. Individuals are free to choose the type of family and role(s) they play within that family according to what suits them best.
- Lone-parent families, single-sex families, child-free families, reconstituted families are all now variations that are part of the fabric of society.
- The traditional two-parent family could be viewed as undesirable because the social construction of gender identity and roles can be a disadvantage for both women and men.
- There is a connection between postmodernism and what has become called 'post-feminism'. Postmodern feminism views women's and men's lives as more open, with choice about the nature of their roles. Women are seen to be able to construct their lives to incorporate being a mother, worker, wife etc. in ways that suit them.

Key concepts

postmodern society; individual choice; fragmented society; diversity; social construction of gender

Key writers

Baudrillard, Hakim, Lyotard

Evaluation

+ The postmodern perspective challenges traditional perspectives on the family and brings a more individualistic approach to what the family means.

+ It tries to apply a more general approach to changes in society to an understanding of family life by introducing concepts such as diversity and choice.
− Doubt could be cast on the ideas of freedom of choice and diversity that postmodernists emphasise, as we are to some extent bound by existing structures and expectations of how we should live.
− Postmodern views are often assertions not based on any real evidence.
− The idea of a 'pick 'n' mix' type of family arrangement is not the norm, because most people prefer stability.

Methods of sociological enquiry and the family

Research into the family has a long history in sociology and social anthropology. Earlier researchers actually lived with and observed the everyday life of their subjects in different cultures from their own. They thought it important to experience the lives of the people they were researching using participant observation. The work of Bronislaw Malinowski (1920s), Margaret Mead (1930s) and Kathleen Gough (1950s and 1960s) provides historical and cross-cultural case study type accounts of the organisation of family life, gender relations and social mores that later sociologists drew upon in their studies of families.

The Young and Willmott legacy — surveys and interviews

Family research in modern sociology has its origins in the work of Young and Willmott in the mid-1950s. These researchers, too, went from their universities to live among and study their subjects — this time to the East End of London — to find out if the extended family still existed. Through the use of interviews and questionnaires, they found a strong, female-headed, working-class extended family still in existence in postwar Britain. Various studies followed the urban renewal programmes of the postwar years where families became dispersed and changed their make-up to become more home-centred and privatised. Young and Willmott's study *The Symmetrical Family* (1973) traced these changes through four stages: (1) the pre-industrial family, (2) the early industrial family, (3) the symmetrical family and (4) the managing director family. At every stage their research involved face-to-face — often semi-structured — interviews with respondents.

In those time, as with other areas of sociology, research was influenced by positivism. Positivists believe that knowledge about the world can be discovered through scientific study. In sociology, the use of quantitative methods to uncover patterns and trends over time was a key feature of research prior to the advent of interpretivism and feminism.

Many studies that followed Young and Willmott focused on family structure, family change, family and kinship. Indeed, Willmott carried out further research in the 1980s in north London, and showed that kinship connections were still in place and important. The terms 'dispersed extended family' and 'beanpole family' have been used to describe these new family structures. As recently as 2000, Willmott was writing about changes in conjugal roles in his book *Complicated Lives*. Finch and Mason (1993) carried out interviews with nearly 1,000 respondents followed by more qualitative in-depth interviewing of 11 kin groups in Manchester, and found that there was still widespread assistance and support among family members.

Numerous criticisms have been levelled at this type of research. It has been claimed that, because of relatively small samples (fewer than 200 managing directors were involved in the Stage 4 family research) and a certain pro-functionalist bias, Young and Willmott's research is flawed. It has been argued that middle-class researchers treated their working-class subjects as 'exotic' or colourful and made statements about their subjects' lives from a middle-class standpoint and a neo-functionalist perspective. Furthermore, researchers are said to have used their students and other researchers to conduct the fieldwork so that they did not actually do much of the research themselves, but rather interpreted the work of their team. Ethical concerns have arisen about how subjects were treated: were they given the opportunity to refuse to take part? And were the respondents 'used' merely to further the academic careers of a new young up-and-coming generation of sociologists?

Feminist research

In the 1970s and 1980s feminists were beginning to challenge the research carried out by 'malestream' sociologists into the nature of the family. Ann Oakley in particular took exception to the so-called 'value-free', 'objective' earlier research. Her work was qualitative, using 'empathetic' techniques, and respondents were treated as equals rather than as subjects of research. Her research on housework, childbirth, childcare and motherhood broke new ground in her personalised accounts of women's feelings and attitudes about their roles in the family. Oakley and others that followed argued strongly that the idea of 'scientific interviewing' meant that no rapport was developed between interviewer and respondent, and as a result the true meaning behind people's lives could not be revealed fully. She argued that any research that broke down the barriers between researcher and subject was preferable to the 'masculine scientific' interviewing.

Hence, there have been differences in the motivation of researchers in their choice of topic to investigate. Choice of topic links with sociological perspective, ethical considerations, practical resources available and the interests of the researcher.

In 2005 Ann Oakley published *The Ann Oakley Reader: Gender, Women and Social Science*, which included edited reprints of her research spanning 40 years into areas of women's lives such as sex and gender, childbirth and motherhood experiences, and family lives. She points to the development of a tradition of feminist research that has qualitative methodology at its centre and has 'elevated' such research strategies in sociology generally. However, she highlights the crucial importance of the formulation of the research question in 'driving the choice of methodological approach'.

Such has been the influence of feminist research that many new aspects of family life have been investigated sociologically for the first time and then become part of the mainstream. An example of this has been the work of Dobash and Dobash (1980), which highlighted the plight of women suffering domestic violence and abuse within the family. More recently sociological debates and research that have been influenced by feminism have included work on relationships and intimacy (Giddens 1992), personal life and social change (Roseneil and Budgeon 2006), teenage parents and parenthood more generally (Duncan 2006), working mothers (Gatrell 2005), the nature of modern childhood (Palmer 2006), sociology and sexuality (Cronin 2006) and gender divisions in an ageing population (Davidson 2006). Much of this research has used qualitative methods (such as case studies, semi-structured interviews, in-depth unstructured interviews) and provided a challenge to conventional thinking about these issues. In particular, the positivist notions of the objective, scientific research have been rejected, not only because of the largely quantitative focus but also because the choice of topics for research often either ignored women or uncritically accepted their traditional roles as wives and mothers.

Research in the 1990s moved on to look at such areas as dual-career families (Dudleston and Owen 1997), conjugal roles and power (Pahl 1993), emotional work in the family (Dunscombe and Marsden 1995), and gay and lesbian households (Dunne 1999 and Stacey 2002). Much of this research has used various types of interviews of a more qualitative nature, such as semi-structured and in-depth interviews.

Much of the early research on the family made assumptions about family life, such as the natural division of labour between women and men and traditional conjugal roles. More recent research is often about how new trends can be understood and explained. It takes into account family diversity, serial monogamy, women working outside the home and changes in childhood.

Primary and secondary methods

Many of these studies have used **primary research** techniques — first-hand methods drawing upon information and evidence gained directly from respondents. However, there is considerable evidence about the nature of family life that has drawn upon **secondary data** — data collected by other researchers, sometimes for other purposes but used by sociologists in their own research. Much of the material is sponsored by the government and is used for social policy development and implementation. The government has its own Office of National Statistics, which analyses and presents information for public use and focuses on many social trends connected with family changes. The Policy Studies Unit, a leading independent research institute, conducts similar research, using questionnaires and interviews.

Examples of secondary sources are *The Labour Force Survey*, *The British Social Attitudes Survey*, *The General Household Survey*, *The Child Development Survey*, *The Census*, parish records (used by Laslett) and *The British Household Panel Survey*. These surveys can involve face-to-face interviews with representative samples from the wider population, but can also use updated statistics related to particular areas. As a result, they can reveal changes in household structure, attitudes to lone parenthood, household patterns and trends, working life, family diversity, ethnicity and family patterns, changes in conjugal roles, gay and lesbian partnerships, changing family roles and changes in parenting styles. They can also show demographic changes over time, as most are conducted at various time intervals and ask similar questions so that results can be compared. Trends and patterns can emerge that sociologists then use in their research to try to understand and explain what is happening.

Note that your own teacher may use different studies from the ones mentioned here.

The family and social policies

Social policies are actions of governments usually in the form of laws that have an impact or effect upon individuals and institutions in society and are often designed to bring about change. Social policies regulate many areas of our family life: there are laws that tell us who we can and cannot marry, when we can get divorced or re-married, how children should be brought up, when we can work and when we can leave home, as well as how we should behave in sexual relationships.

Historically, the government made laws and introduced social policies that affected the family — for example, the Factory and Child Labour Acts in the nineteenth century prevented the employment of children and women. The Child Support Agency is a more recent example of the government trying to ensure that absent parents (often fathers) meet their financial responsibilities to their children.

There are now many social policies surrounding conception, pregnancy, abortion, childbirth, child-rearing and infancy. Education, early adulthood, adulthood and old age are governed by social policies. The family is a major institution influenced by social policies.

Perspectives on social policy

Marxist

There are two Marxist views about the nature and role of social policy in a capitalist society:

(1) Some Marxists believe that social policies help to maintain the status quo. The same class — the bourgeoisie — runs the economy and the government, and makes the laws. By making it seem that capitalism can solve social problems such as poverty, educational underachievement or anti-social behaviour and make society a better place, criticism is reduced. This will have the effect of dampening any rebellious or revolutionary action by the working class that may threaten the status quo.

(2) Other Marxists believe that social policies are concessions from the ruling class (bourgeoisie) won by the working class (proletariat) through strikes and protests in order to improve their lives. The capitalist class makes improvements to the lives of the working class because it realises the need to appear receptive to demands for change. This preserves the ideology of capitalism and prevents criticism or conflict that may threaten to undermine the system.

New Right

Although certain social policies are necessary to support the family, the New Right sees some changes as undermining the traditional family structure. These writers often disagree strongly with providing benefits for single parents or making divorce easier for couples, because they want to preserve the view that the hetereosexual, nuclear family is the best form of the family.

Feminist

Many feminists believe that social policies support an ideology of 'familism'. This means that policies are directed at supporting a particular type of family that consists of two parents and their children. Policies support the notion of the traditional roles of men and women in the family and encourage the ideology of women's natural role as wives/mothers/carers and men's role as breadwinners.

> **Key concepts**
>
> Marxist: the state; status quo; ideological state apparatus; social class; social control
> New Right: nanny state; traditional family values
> Feminist: ideology of familism; patriarchal values

Changing patterns of marriage, cohabitation, separation, divorce, child-bearing and the life course

Key ideas

The following points are a summary of the important changes that have taken place in key aspects of the family and household structures. You should be able to discuss different views on both the causes and the consequences of these changes. A grasp of the statistical evidence regarding changing patterns of marriage and divorce, family size and changing trends in child-bearing will provide you with a good basis for going on to understand the explanations for these changes. But first, make sure you have a sound knowledge of concepts such as 'cohabitation' and 'life course', as well as the following terms:

- **monogamy** — marriage between one woman and one man at a time
- **polygamy** — the general term used to describe marriage between more than one of either sex at a time, with **polyandry** meaning marriage between one woman and more than one man at a time, and **polygyny** meaning marriage between one man and more than one woman at a time
- **endogamy** — marriage within the same tribe, ethnic group or social class
- **exogamy** — marriage outside the tribe, ethnic group or social class

Marriage and cohabitation

- While there has been a fall in the marriage rate and a growth in cohabitation, marriage is still the most common form of partnership between men and women. In 2004/05 half of men and women were married, while only one in ten was cohabiting.

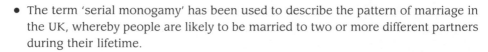

- The term 'serial monogamy' has been used to describe the pattern of marriage in the UK, whereby people are likely to be married to two or more different partners during their lifetime.

Separation and divorce

- Divorce is defined as the legal termination of marriage, and the divorce rate is usually expressed as the number of divorces in any one year per 1,000 married couples in the population. About 40% of marriages will end in divorce. Separation is another form of marital breakdown and is difficult to measure as some couples live apart informally, so there are no reliable statistical data.
- The divorce rate increased following a number of legal changes in the twentieth century — particularly after the implementation of the Divorce Reform Act in 1971. However, in 2005 there was an 8% fall in the divorce rate to 13% per 1,000 of the married population.
- Women are more likely than men to petition for divorce and have a divorce granted to them.
- The main reasons given for the increase in divorce include: the legal changes, which make divorce easier, simpler, quicker and cheaper; changing attitudes to divorce (less of a stigma); growing expectations of marriage, particularly for women; the growing independence of women; the influence of feminist ideas related to fulfilment in marriage; the isolation of the nuclear family from relatives who could provide support; growing financial and work pressures on many couples and families; secularisation and the decline in the influence of the Church.

Changes in family structure

- There has been a growth in 'reconstituted' or 'reordered' families following divorce and remarriage. Since 1981, one in ten divorcing men and women had had a previous marriage that also ended in divorce. One in four children lives in a lone-parent household, usually headed by a woman.
- The two most common reasons for heading a lone-parent household are (i) single lone motherhood (women who have never married or cohabited and who have children) and (ii) divorce or separation where the children stay with their mother. However, the figures on the proportions living in single-parent families should be viewed as a *snapshot* of the situation at any one point in time. Many individuals may spend some of their time in single-parent homes, but not all of their life. Hence, single-parent families, for many, are a temporary occurrence between changes or realignments in family arrangements.
- There has been a rise in the numbers of 'singletons' (people living on their own), a large proportion of whom are pensioners. Single-person households include:
  - young people who choose to live alone
  - divorced or separated people who are still on their own
  - pensioners living alone (increasing life expectancy, especially for women, has added to the number of elderly widowed people living alone)
- There has been an increase in the number of 'empty-nest' families as children grow up and leave home. However, there is evidence of older children and

particularly sons returning to or staying in the family home until a later age because of the cost of getting access to the housing market.

Child-bearing
- The fertility rate has fallen, leading to smaller families, and there has been a growth in childless and child-free couples ('child-free' is the term used to describe women or couples who choose not to have children). In 2001 the fertility rate was 1:64 children per woman of child-bearing age. This means that fertility has fallen below the rate to keep the population size stable (this excludes migration factors, which also affect population size). There has been an increase in the average age of women at the time of the birth of their first child to 29.
- The reasons for the decline in the fertility rate and the increase in the average age of motherhood include: the fall in the infant mortality rate; greater availability of reliable and safe contraception; later marriage; the high cost of raising children; the increase in the number of women in higher education; more and better employment prospects for women; changes in women's perception of their role.
- There is a high rate of teenage single parenthood and a decline in the stigma of being a lone parent, particularly an unmarried mother.

Diversity of family and household structures
Ethnic variations
- There are important variations in relation to families and households of South Asian heritage. Men and women are more likely to marry earlier, have high rates of marriage and arranged marriages (especially among Muslims and Sikhs), and low rates of separation and divorce, although there has been a slight increase in the divorce rate in this group.
- Higher fertility rates have been found among Pakistani and Bangladeshi women. Their families are likely to be larger, with the women as full-time mothers and family arrangements more patriarchal. They are likely to have grandparents or other kin living with them — usually the husband's parents.
- Families of black Caribbean heritage have low rates of marriage, high levels (43%) of single parenthood (usually female), and high rates of separation and divorce.

Class variations
- There are class variations in families and households too: the traditional working-class family is more likely to have segregated conjugal roles, closer kinship networks and patriarchal family arrangements.
- The middle-class family is more likely to have joint conjugal roles, with the woman in full-time paid employment. It is described by Young and Willmott as 'symmetrical' and has a privatised focus on home and childcare. However, qualitative research by Ann Oakley questions this view of the family.

'Privatisation' of family
- The 'privatisation' of the family, especially in relation to social class, has also been an area of study for sociologists. Finch and Mason (1989) challenge the view of the isolated, privatised nuclear family in their research, using interviews and follow-up qualitative research with kin groups, in Manchester.

Extended family

- There has been a shift to smaller, more isolated nuclear families with less face-to-face contact with relatives, although many families keep in contact by phone, internet, e-mail or at times of important family events such as birthdays, weddings etc. Hence, it may be that the nature of being an extended family has changed rather than the concept disappeared.
- Families whose heritage is linked to the Indian subcontinent and Cypriot families keep close contact with their wider family. As noted above, they may also be more likely to have extended kin living in the same household. They tend to marry young and remain living with relatives.

There are considerable variations in the life-course experience of individuals that are unique to them. Life-course research suggests that experiences throughout life are unpredictable, or less predictable than the typical life cycle through birth, child-hood, adolescence, marriage, children, empty nest, old age and death may indicate. Each aspect of the cycle is different, depending upon a number of factors, the most important of which could be social class, gender and ethnicity, but could also include education, work experience, income and wealth.

Key concepts

marriage rate; divorce rate; reconstituted families; reordered families; cohabitation; childless/child-free; family size; privatised family; conjugal roles; kinship networks; fertility rate; serial monogamy; marital breakdown; securalisation

Gender roles, domestic labour and power relationships

Key ideas

- Roles in the family have been linked to the move from extended to nuclear families, with men and women developing more specialised roles after industrialisation. Evidence underpins the argument that women still spend more time than men doing and taking much more responsibility for domestic arrangements. Feminists have argued that the socialisation of children plays a large part in teaching them their expected roles in the family: males as breadwinners, females as wives and mothers. Even though women now are also breadwinners, they still take on most domestic labour in the family.
- In the mid-1960s Hannah Gavron conducted research using unstructured inter-views to compare the domestic arrangements of working- and middle-class young mothers. She found that there seemed to be more shared conjugal roles and sharing of tasks around the home than before, but some young mothers also felt the 'capitivity' of marriage. Gavron noted that at the time of her study women were beginning to have higher expectations about marriage and life generally.

- Research by Young and Willmott in 1975 suggested that men and women were beginning to play more equal conjugal roles in the family and that a 'symmetrical family' was emerging. However, research by feminists such as Ann Oakley questioned the validity of the research and found evidence that contested this view. It seems particularly evident that when women have children, even if there was equality in domestic arrangements before, their roles revert to a traditional pattern.
- Evidence from the *British Attitudes Survey* has shown that housework and child-care are still gendered activities. Women still carry out the mundane, ongoing domestic activities like washing, cleaning, cooking, shopping etc., while men may be more likely to be involved in the more 'creative' activities such as repair work and playing with children. Research by Dunscombe and Marsden (1995) has pointed to the important but often hidden emotional 'work' women do in the family by maintaining the illusion of having satisfactory family relationships by 'living the family myth'.
- Gatrell (2005), drawing on her qualitative study, found mothers in employment still experiencing discrimination at work and predictably still undertaking most of the housework.
- Power relationships in the family have been characterised by feminist sociologists as patriarchal, with men having most of the decision-making power over their wives and children. Early sociological studies by Young and Willmott of the extended working-class families in the East End of London, by Henriques and Slaughter of mining families and by Tunstall of families of deep-sea fishermen painted a picture of the separate lives of men and women — men being predom-inantly breadwinners with little input into the family and childcare, and women being predominantly housewives and mothers, although even these early studies often recognise the matriarchal power of women through the role of the oldest mother figure in the family (Mum), who had significant control and power in family organisation.
- Recent research has pointed to the development of a 'modified extended family' arrangement rather than the privatised nuclear family. Roseneil and Budgeon used in-depth, qualitative interviews to provide insight into people's emotional lives. They found friends to be an increasingly significant part of everyday lives, to such an extent that they could be called the 'new family'. But the main observation is that there is considerable family and household diversity in terms of conjugal roles and power structures. One of the most important changes to have affected family structure in the twentieth century is the greater participation of married women in the workforce. This has led to a change in attitudes about the roles of men, women and children. However, the Office of National Statistics indicates that in 2002 women still spent twice as long as men on housework each day.
- There has been a change in the way that research into conjugal roles and the domestic division of labour has been carried out. Older research tended to be quantitative and relied on the statistical results of interviews and the assumption of heterosexual norms (**heteronormativity**). Recent work takes a more qualitative approach and explores in depth complex issues and perceptions about family life

and roles. Domestic tasks are not simply carried out like 'jobs' but relate to conceptions of masculinity and femininity and how our identities are formed.

Key terms

segregated/joint conjugal role; industrialisation; urbanisation; symmetrical family; emotional work; women's dual role; nuclear family; extended family; modified extended family; socialisation; heteronormativity; domestic division of labour

Key writers

Dunscombe and Marsden, Edgell, Gatrell, Gavron, Giddens, Oakley, Ramos, Roseneil and Budgeon, Young and Willmott,

Useful website

www.nationalstatistics.org

Childhood and changes in the status of children

Key ideas

Social construction of childhood

- Evidence from the past and from other cultures shows that what a society considers to be 'childhood' varies and is not merely based on age or biological/psychological maturity.
- Childhood is socially constructed by adults. Children are defined as such and there are expectations and attitudes attached to how children should behave and be treated.
- Notions of childhood have changed over time. In the past, children 'needed' to be controlled by adults to stop them turning evil.
- Childhood today is often viewed as a time of innocence, vulnerability and dependence when adults are responsible for the care and protection of children. Adults working with children (such as teachers) must undergo a police check to make sure they have no convictions for child abuse (this check is called an 'enhanced disclosure').

Changes in children's legal rights

- There have been changes in the legal rights of children in terms of employment, education, crime and abuse which are linked to prevailing views of children and childhood. It is now frowned upon to hit a child, whereas this was commonplace in the past and institutionalised in schools with corporal punishment. 'Age patriarchy' is a term used to describe the power and control that adults have over the lives of children.

Differences between societies

- In other societies children work long hours — often in appalling conditions for low wages. Some aspects of the way children are treated at work have been described as slavery in that children have no control or choice over their work.
- In addition, many children have responsibilities for caring for younger siblings or even maintaining a family, which we might consider too difficult for children of such a young age.
- In societies with a high rate of HIV/AIDS, many children are orphaned and left to care for other members of their families at a young age or are brought up by elderly grandparents.
- Another aspect of childhood in war-torn countries is that some children are forced to become soldiers and are brutalised into killing people.

Prolonged childhood

- It has been argued that there are developments that further compartmentalise childhood, such as the advent of the 'tweenie' (a young teenager), which is probably linked to the advertising market and is used as a marketing tool.
- On the other hand, teenagers of 15 or 16 years of age are sometimes described as children — boys or girls — when in other societies they would be considered as adults.

Shortened childhood

- There is another view that there has been a blurring of the boundaries between childhood and adulthood. Children, particularly girls, are dressed in 'sexualised' clothes from a young age and the mass media market a range of goods that could be seen as exploiting children as consumers.
- It has been suggested that there has been 'loss of innocence' through exposure to 'adult' issues such as sex and death through the mass media and, increasingly, the internet and weblogs. Those intent on the abuse of children are increasingly getting access to children through the web as many other avenues have been closed through greater security and vigilance.

Central role of children in the family

- Children in the West are now the focus of family life, whereas in the past the old adage was 'children should be seen and not heard'.

Key concepts

social construction of childhood; age patriarchy

Key writers

Aries, Berger and Berger, Bernardes, Foucault, Postman, Taylor

Useful websites

www.un.org
www.unicef.org

Child abuse

- Children suffer cruelty from adults, and each week one child dies as a result of injuries caused by their parents or carers (Office of National Statistics 1998–2001).
- Children are most likely to be abused by someone in their family or someone they know.
- There is a child protection register that alerts social workers to children who are in vulnerable circumstances — it contains approximately 30,000 names.
- According to the national Children's Bureau, in 2007 hospitals in England treated 471 children each week who had sustained deliberate injuries.
- Every Child Matters is an initiative to bring together all agencies that deal with children — schools, police, hospitals, social workers — to prevent abuse of children from being undetected. It arose as the result of the death of 8-year-old Victoria Climbie who was abused and killed by her aunt.

Key terms

demography; fertility rate; birth rate; infant mortality rate; death rate; economic burden; economic asset

Key writers

Chester; Leach, Allan and Crow; Rapoport and Rapoport

Useful sources of information

British Social Attitudes Survey; General Household Survey; Labour Force Survey

Demographic trends in the UK since 1900

Key ideas

Demography is the study of population statistics and trends or changes in population size and structure.

Important definitions

- **Fertility rate** — the number of live births per 1,000 women of child-bearing age (15–44) in the population per year.
- **Birth rate (crude)** — the number of live births per 1,000 of the population per year.
- **Death rate** — the number of deaths per 1,000 of the population per year.
- **Infant mortality rate** — the number of deaths of infants under 1 year of age per 1,000 live births per year.

Make a careful note of the difference between the fertility rate and the birth rate. The fertility rate is expressed as a ratio. A ratio of 1:79 means 1.79 children per woman of child-bearing age. This was the 2005 figure, compared with 1.63, a record low, in

2001. The fertility rate in 2006 was the highest for 6 years at 1.87. The rise in the fertility rate (going against an overall downward trend as you will see below) has been explained by older women in their 40s having more than two children. This could be because there are better maternity/paternity benefits and increasing accept-ance of flexible working arrangements to accommodate parents (they now have the right to request these if they have children under the age of 16) but also because fertility treatment increases the chance of multiple births. The influx of younger migrants is expected to have an impact on the fertility rate as well.

The crude birth rate is also expressed as a ratio, but per 1,000 of the whole popula-tion (including men and children), so 55:1000 means 55 births per 1,000 people in a given year.

The population of Britain is ageing because life expectancy is increasing. Life expectancy is higher in the higher social classes. By 2020 it is expected that half the population will be over 50.

Reasons for general decline in fertility and birth rate
- The widespread availability of reliable contraception has enabled people to plan their fertility more easily than in the past.
- There is growing childlessness among particular groups of women — such as highly qualified women.
- With the decline in the infant mortality rate, and as more of the children born survive into adulthood, women need to have fewer children overall.
- The cost of having children and raising them means that children are no longer an economic asset.
- Women are going out to work.
- There is a change in attitudes to family size.
- Women are delaying having children and focusing on their careers.

Reasons for the overall decline of the death rate
- improvements in medical knowledge, medicine and health care
- improvements in health and safety at work
- better diet and environmental living conditions/sanitation
- vaccination programmes such polio and the MMR vaccine
- better housing conditions and less overcrowding
- improved maternity and antenatal care

These population statistics vary with class and ethnicity. The working class has higher death rates, infant mortality rates, birth rates and fertility rates than the middle class. This is also true for many other indicators of health and illness such as cancer rates and even accident rates. Some ethnic groups have higher rates of fertility, infant mortality, and death rates than the average, such as those of Pakistani heritage.

Reasons for the decline in family size
- widespread use and reliability of contraception
- women working outside the home having careers — changing attitudes towards women's role in the family

- changing attitudes — smaller families more desirable
- cost of having a large family
- no longer an economic need for children — economic burden rather than economic asset

Useful websites

www.opcs.gov.uk
www.statistics.gov.uk

Questions
&
Answers

This section of the guide provides you with six typical AQA exam questions on the topic of **Families and Households**. The first five have an answer that would achieve an A grade if written in the unit test. However, *do not* learn the answer and think you will be able to reproduce it in the exam. Treat the answers as a *possible* way to approach the question. There are other answers that could also achieve an A grade. Pay particular attention to where marks are gained and the style of the answer. Three of the questions also have a C-grade answer so that you can gauge the difference between the two levels.

Remember that you are marked on making use of relevant material, showing accurate and comprehensive knowledge and understanding, referring to studies where appropriate and making use of suitable sociological concepts. You will gain higher marks if you can display critical, analytical and evaluative skills — showing that you know the strengths and weaknesses of arguments, accounts, explanations and theories. If your work is also logical and well structured, particularly the (d) and (e) questions, this will go a long way to ensuring a good grade.

The sixth question is for you try by yourself without the support of a student answer. Some guidance is given to help you answer it correctly.

Examiner's comments

The answers to the first five questions are followed by comments from an examiner, indicated by the *e* icon. These comments explain where and how marks have been gained. The comments on the grade-A answer pay particular attention to where there is clear evidence of the skills — knowledge and understanding, application, interpretation, analysis and evaluation — being displayed with relevance to the question. The comments on the grade-C answer point to errors, problems and areas where there is room for improvement.

Domestic violence, the roles of women and men and the family

Read Items 2A and 2B below and answer parts (a) to (e) that follow.

Item 2A

Every year approximately 120 women are killed by violent partners. They have often suffered a history of abuse over several years. Some complain to the police, while others suffer in silence. The British Crime Survey has shown that 50% of all adult women say that they have experienced some sort of domestic violence, sexual assault or stalking. However, the men who abuse — and sometimes even murder — their partner are often treated leniently by the courts.

Professors Rebecca and Russell Dobash have led research in the field of domestic abuse and violence over many years. They have used in-depth, informal interview techniques with the victims of violence to research this often hidden crime against women. Their findings show that marriage is often a power relationship that reflects the inequality between men and women in the wider society. It is the power held by men and the dependence of women that can trigger attacks on women.

Item 2B

There have been many changes in society that have led to greater equality between men and women. However, some sociologists have argued that power relations in the family are still unequal. When studying conjugal roles, decision-making, control over finance, and dual-career households, researchers have found evidence that in the majority of households 'men still wear the trousers' and are the main decision-makers and breadwinners. The greater number of women in paid employment in the workforce, however, has been shown to bring about a move towards greater equality in financial management of the family but not overall equality between partners.

(a) Give *one* reason why men who abuse their partner might be treated leniently by the courts (Item 2A). (2 marks)

(b) Suggest *two* explanations for the fact that domestic violence is often a 'hidden crime' (Item 2A). (4 marks)

(c) Identify *three* reasons why domestic violence might be a difficult area for sociologists to study. (6 marks)

question

(d) **Discuss the value of the use of qualitative techniques of research such as in-depth interviews in understanding domestic violence (Item 2A).** (24 marks)

(e) **Using material from the Items and elsewhere, assess the view that there are still unequal power relationships between men and women in society.** (24 marks)

■ ■ ■

Answer to question 1: grade-C candidate

(a) The courts treat violence against women as not real violence and then men get away with it.

    There is not sufficient clarity or detail to gain 2 marks — 1 mark is awarded for some recognition that the courts do not take violence against women seriously.

(b) A woman may think there is no point in reporting violence she has suffered as nothing will be done about it because the police don't take it seriously. Also women tend to blame themselves for causing the violence by doing something to annoy their partners.

    Two appropriate reasons are given — 4 marks.

(c) It is difficult to study domestic violence because it is a private area of family life, people don't talk openly about it and it is difficult for sociologists to get access to victims of such crimes.

    There are three reasons here but the first two are really making the same point. The third reason is appropriate, so 2 + 2 marks are awarded — 4 marks in total. It is helpful, to both you and the examiner, if the answers to questions such as this are listed as bullet points.

(d) Qualitative methods are used by sociologists when they want to gain in-depth and detailed information about an area of social life in their research. In-depth interviews and observations are techniques that have been strongly associated with the interactionist perspective and more recently feminism. Hence, the development of such methods of research is associated with a particular theoretical view of society. Interactionism is based on the idea that individuals create society and give meaning to their lives through their actions and reactions to their social circumstances. To study society, therefore, sociologists must find ways of seeing the world through the respondent's eyes, they must take sides.

    This is a clearly written paragraph and shows a good understanding of qualitative methods and theoretical links. However, no mention has been made of the subject matter of the question. It is acceptable to write an introduction such as this, but you must make sure that your next paragraph begins to answer the question set.

    Task Try to think of an opening sentence that would have been relevant to the question, but would also have allowed the student to write the rest of the introduction as it is above.

Domestic violence is one of those areas which is largely hidden from view. Women who are the victims of violence often hide the abuse and certainly don't openly talk about it. Researchers like Dobash and Dobash have found that women often blame themselves for causing the violence too. Therefore sociologists would be limited if they used structured questionnaires or other quantitative methods or tried to be scientific in their approach because they would only be scratching the surface of this complicated, personal issue. Using in-depth interviews allows the interviewer to gain the trust of the respondent, putting them at ease and getting them to talk at length about their experience. The interviewer can empathise with the respondent and if the characteristics of the respondent are matched with the researcher in terms of age, gender and ethnicity this can make the respondent feel more at ease.

This paragraph shows knowledge and understanding of in-depth interviews and how they can be used in research into sensitive topics. There is some awareness of other methods and their weaknesses. There is also an awareness of the importance of the role of the interviewer. Some of the points being made are general and could be used to relate more overtly to domestic violence.

In-depth interviews are known to paint a richer picture of social life and get under the surface and find out what is really going on. Such interviews can also provide a detailed picture. The respondent provides an account of their world from their own experience of it and it will therefore be more likely to provide an accurate account than someone watching from outside. This is what Dobash and Dobash have done in their research. They have found all sorts of evidence of the unequal power relationships between men and women in marriage. They have found that men use violence and the threat of violence as a form of control over their wives. Other interactionists like Becker and feminists like Oakley have put in-depth interviews into practice in other areas like deviance and housework.

So, in-depth interviews and qualitative methods generally can be used by sociologists to study areas of life and issues which are difficult to find out about using other techniques.

While this student has discussed the value of in-depth interviews and qualitative techniques generally, there has been no mention in the answer of possible disadvantages or weaknesses of these methods. The answer shows a reasonable knowledge and understanding of the topic, though the relevance of the material to the question is not always made explicit. By looking only at the strengths of qualitative techniques, the answer is one-sided and fails to gain many of the potential analysis and evaluation marks that are available. The conclusion is weak and ineffectual. Overall, this answer gains 12 marks out of 24.

Task Write down as many disadvantages of using qualitative methods, such as in-depth interviews, that you can think of, and then identify which aspects would be relevant to this question.

question

(e) Feminists point out that we still live in a patriarchal society where men and women still have unequal power. This inequality affects all areas of society from within the family, the world of work and promotion, education, the law. Even in relationships women are at a disadvantage and can be the victims of violence as stated in Item 2A.

>  This opening paragraph shows an implicit understanding of a key and relevant concept — patriarchy — and gives some examples of where unequal power relationships exist. It would have been helpful to name one or two feminists who have made the point about our patriarchal society.

The inequalities women experience today link back to Victorian times when women could not own property, were themselves owned by men — husbands, fathers. Fathers still symbolically 'give away' their daughters on their wedding day. Women did not get the right to vote until 1928. Their divorce rights were given long after they were given to men.

> A short but significant historical context. This needs to be brief, as it is, since it is only marginally relevant to the question. It is usually best to keep to contemporary issues and material unless explicitly stated otherwise in the question.

Women have gained from many changes in the law and now have equal rights at work, they must be paid equally for doing work of 'equal value' to men. Discrimination based on sex is also illegal. However, on average women still earn less than men because they take time off to have children and are more likely to work part time.

> This is good, relevant material but would benefit from greater detail and expansion. Evidence from research and feminist perspectives would strengthen this section.

Women still suffer domestic violence as stated in the Items and this can be seen as an expression of men's patriarchal control in society. Although they may be getting more equality in other areas, this is still a fact of many women's lives. Education is the big success story for many girls and women. GCSE and A-level results are better for females than males and more women are in higher education than men. Women have higher expectations for their lives today than their mothers or their grandmothers had.

> **The reference to the Items is cursory and should have been occurring throughout the answer — not just in the first and last sections. When a question refers you to the Items, there will always be useful and important information in them that you can use to develop your answer. This answer generally benefits from showing knowledge and understanding and this is where the majority of the marks are gained, but there is little reference to research and evidence. There is some evaluation in the recognition that there are arguments for and against the view that there are still unequal power relationships between men**

and women, but it is not sufficiently detailed or explicit enough to gain many marks. Further evaluation could have been shown by raising the question of whether all women suffer to the same degree from unequal power relationships. There is also the issue that while unequal power relationships affect everyone to some degree, only some men abuse their wives physically — suggesting that other factors might also be at work. This answer would gain 12 marks out of 24.

Overall mark: 33/60

■ ■ ■

Answer to question 1: grade-A candidate

(a) As we live in a patriarchal society in which men have most of the power, violence against women is often seen as less serious than other forms of violence, and this is reflected in the attitude of the courts.

🖉 This gets across the point that in a society where men have most of the power and authority there is an attitude in society that views attacks on women as less important than other forms of violence — 'just a domestic'. The answer is short and to the point and gains 2 marks.

(b) One reason is that women do not report cases of domestic violence to the police because they are frightened of their partner and worry that the abuse might get worse. Another reason is that the women often blame themselves for the violence. They therefore don't like to talk about it to anyone.

🖉 The candidate gives two clear reasons. There is no need to go into further detail of these reasons at this stage because the question does not require a development — 4 marks.

Other reasons that might have been offered include:
- No confidence in the police to stop the violence.
- Only recently included as a separate category in the crime rate/statistics.
- Women feel ashamed to report it.

(c) People, especially women, often don't want to talk about domestic violence because it is a sensitive topic and shows their family life is in a mess. There are problems with getting access to victims of domestic violence as there is no single list of people who have experienced or committed domestic violence. There would be a need to use qualitative research techniques to study this topic and you would need to use trained researchers. It would take a lot of time to get people to speak freely and openly and it would, therefore, be expensive.

🖉 The candidate is given 1 mark each for three reasons (the personal, sensitive nature of the crime, getting access to the victim and the use of in-depth methods) and a further mark each for explaining each one more fully. In a 6-mark question the marks are usually broken down into three reasons × 2 marks for each reason plus some

further detail. This answer gives three good reasons why sociologists might find the topic difficult to study, and each is elaborated sufficiently to gain the second mark for each point. Note that it is acceptable in questions such as this to make your answer as a bullet-pointed list. This shows each of the points separately and clearly.

(d) Sociologists have used qualitative methods when they want to get a deeper picture of what is happening, get under the surface and find out how people see and experience things themselves. Although these methods can take a long time and cost a lot of money, they get better results that are more valid.

> This is a short but good opening paragraph with words that will trigger a positive response from the examiner ('deeper picture', 'under the surface', 'how people see and experience things themselves', 'valid'). It would have been even better if the term 'valid' had been explained, to show that the student understood its meaning and could identify what might be considered as being less valid than qualitative methods. There is some evaluation in the last sentence about time and cost, showing that the student has an awareness of weaknesses as well as strengths. Note that there has been no mention of domestic violence yet — this needs to appear soon as it is the main point of the question.

> **Tip** Always keep the question uppermost in your mind. Go back and reread it after every paragraph you write to make sure everything you are writing is explicitly relevant.

Domestic violence is a hidden crime and it is difficult to get any detailed information about it from the police or other official sources as it is classified as confidential. However, sociologists can get statistics on it because the courts and police have to keep records which then become public documents, i.e. official statistics. But these just scratch the surface and tell sociologists about the numbers, not the stories behind the numbers. Quantitative methods like statistics are often used by positivists because they believe that things that happen in the world can be measured as social facts in a scientific way. Durkheim did this with his study of suicide and found it had a social cause. The same is true of domestic violence. However, to really understand the meaning behind it like Dobash and Dobash you must try to understand from the victim's point of view and it can be interesting from the abuser's angle as well. This is why qualitative methods are better. The sociologist can get the trust of the person, have empathy with them, allow them to tell their story in detail. Before the research carried out by Dobash and Dobash the topic of domestic violence was not really talked about or understood. They helped change views about it and the police and society now take it more seriously.

> The first part of this paragraph is rather muddled. The student has lost sight of the question. However, there are some good points that just need to be made more clearly. Using the positivist perspective could have been put to better use by making explicit that it is a criticism of the qualitative approach — an evaluative comment lost. The second part of the paragraph gets back on track by referring to the Item and beginning to discuss the advantages of in-depth interviews.

> **Tip** Assume you are writing your answer for someone who is not as familiar with the material as you and imagine you are trying to explain the answer to them for the first time. Do not assume the examiner will 'read into' what you are saying. He or she will read the words on the page and mark accordingly. Show that you know what terms mean and make it clear why you have chosen to put something down in your answer.

Feminists and interactionists are keen to use qualitative methods like in-depth interviews to get a realistic understanding of how people's lives are lived. Ann Oakley has shown how informal and sensitive questioning and discussion can reveal a considerable amount about the respondent's experience. Oakley argues that qualitative methods such as in-depth interviews make the barriers between the research and person less threatening especially if the people are similar, i.e. same gender. Feminists believe that, like society, sociology is male-dominated and that rather than being like a science of society, sociology should see life through the eyes of the person being studied. Becker said this too: he thought sociology should be about seeing the world through the eyes of the person being studied. Feminists like Roberts also believe it's important to study women's lives and how they experience life because before, much of the positivist research was about men — this is called patriarchy. So using in-depth interviews is about getting a rich picture, a true-to-life picture and a lot of detail. But it is also about seeing society in the meaning that people give to their experiences and lives, seeing things from their point of view and empathising with them. Interactionists also use observation to study people but this would not be ethical for domestic violence because it's a crime. Also it would not be possible to get at what domestic violence is really like using other methods and find out how women feel about being mistreated and abused. Dobash and Dobash found that women often blame themselves and think they caused the violence until they escape from it.

However, there are also problems with the use of qualitative methods that positivist sociologists would put forward to justify the use of traditional forms of research like surveys, structured questionnaires and interviews. They would argue that qualitative research is open to interpretation and you can never be fully sure that you have understood the meaning behind an answer or comment from a respondent. There is always the subjectivity in the use of such methods and this means that validity can be compromised. Also because large amounts of data are collected it is not possible to quantify and categorise the outcomes of the research in tables, charts or graphs to illustrate trends and patterns of behaviour. It is also difficult to repeat qualitative research to check the results were accurate, which positivists also find a failing with such methods.

> ℯ Some good points are made and developed. Marks are gained for bringing in perspectives that are correct. Linking the methods to views about society and the use of appropriate concepts all gain marks, as does showing a reasonable understanding of the feminist perspective and its impact on sociology, although the term 'patriarchy' could have been explained more clearly. The second paragraph gets the

essay back on track and makes relevant connections to the question. If you read each sentence, you should be able to see that each could have been further elaborated with extra detail. The last section, which provides some criticisms of the use of qualitative methods, shows the candidate's evaluative skills.

In conclusion, subjects like domestic violence couldn't be studied in as much depth using traditional methods like questionnaires and surveys as it's too personal to get any solid information about using structured questionnaires and statistics. Qualitative methods see the world through the eyes of the individual involved. It is interpretivists or action theorists who believe that we create our own lives and understand what is going on through our own eyes in particular contexts. Therefore, to really understand the world, sociologists have to use in-depth interviews or observation to get at what is really going on under the surface and see life through the eyes of those who are living it. Men who beat up their wives are part of a patriarchal society that says men can have control over women and dominate them, even physically through rape and violence. Domestic violence in the home can be hidden but is just another way for men to make sure they have control over their partners/wives. Dobash and Dobash and other feminists like Oakley have discovered this through qualitative research. Therefore, the use of in-depth interviews has been invaluable in understanding domestic violence. It has given us detailed evidence about the nature and extent of violence from an individual woman's point of view as well as within a societal context. The use of traditional sociological methods would provide statistical evidence based on official figures but would not be able to provide the depth.

🖉 **This is a good concluding section which draws together the practical and theoretical advantages of using qualitative methods to study seemingly hidden aspects of our lives. It uses and explains the feminist perspective to good effect and sets the context for its role in sociology, specifically understanding women's lives. Overall, this answer would gain 20 marks out of 24.**

To gain 24 marks, the answer would have to develop some points in more detail — for example, go into more depth and particularly display evaluation skills that indicate some more of the disadvantages of qualitative research. There would have to be more clarity, especially in the section on positivism.

(e) As Item 2B shows, domestic violence is usually committed by men against women although there are a small number of reported cases of women being violent against men. In the past it was not illegal for a husband to hit his wife. It was believed that it was the husband's right to control his family and have power over them. Also men were seen as breadwinners and their role more important than women's roles as wives and mothers. This was true in Victorian times and is still believed by some people even though most women are now in employment. Although women have more rights today, men still have most of the power.

✐ This opening paragraph sets the historical scene and shows an understanding of how the past may influence our attitudes and views today. The two traditionally distinct roles of men and women are described too. Reference is made to Item 2B.

As reports by the Equal Opportunities Commission have shown, today men still earn more than women and more often carry on full-time work when the couple have children, whereas women often give up work or go into part-time employment. Women often have to fit work in around childcare and therefore are more likely to work part time or give up work for a period of time. This gives men more control over finances and decisions and puts them in a more powerful position. This then makes men more confident in other areas and makes women seem more subordinate or secondary. Although this might not lead directly to domestic violence, as Item A states over 50% of women have experienced some sort of violence or stalking and young women are more vulnerable than older women.

There is a general attitude that comes from the dominance of men in industry, the media, sport and politics that they have more choice in what they do and how they behave. They have more independence and can act according to their own interests and desires. Indeed sociologists such as McRobbie have argued that much of our perceptions and images of the world, especially through the media, are from a 'male gaze'. This is an ideology which sees women as secondary, as objects, and treats their lives as less important than men's. The culture of 'femininity' has socialised some women into thinking that 'getting a partner' is their key aim in life and therefore the associated culture of 'romantic love' has become the dominant focus in many women's lives. Marxist feminists would point out that the major divisions between men and women in society will remain the same as long as there is a capitalist system in place. There may be improvements in the distribution of power but men will essentially remain in powerful positions at work and at home.

✐ This is quite a wide-ranging paragraph that makes some important key points. Violence is linked to a general attitude about the relationships of men and women and hence ties in nicely with the previous paragraph. Links are made to the Items and then elaborated. Other research and perspectives are brought in that are relevant to understanding the effect of a particular ideology on women themselves. Even more evaluation would have been shown if the answer had pointed out the Marxist view that, because of the class system, some men have much more power and freedom of choice than others.

However, as pointed out in Item 2B there are other areas where women have gained equality such as in education. Girls and boys follow the same curriculum and now girls get better results than boys, and over half of undergraduates are female, but choice of subject post-16 is still quite traditional with more boys doing science and maths and more girls doing arts subjects. In law women have equality and the Equal Pay and Sex Discrimination Acts have brought about improvements in women's working lives. There is evidence that women are gaining better managerial positions than in the past and maintaining a career as well as having families. There is more respect for women in society and women see themselves in a more positive light these days. Many of them want careers and good pay too. All of these changes have had an impact upon women's family life. Sometimes women see their jobs as even more important than having a family. There is evidence in national statistics that some highly qualified women decide not to have children at all.

However, in many areas of society generally men have more power than women. This is called patriarchy and has been extensively researched. Feminists in particular have provided evidence of how men are dominant — this starts from childhood during socialisation into sex roles. Boys are encouraged to be outgoing, independent, to hide their emotions, while girls are encouraged to play with dolls, help Mum with the housework and stay closer to home. Men's roles are seen as more important than women's. Once in a relationship women often become secondary to men, especially when they have children. The status of wife and mother is low compared with the breadwinner. The legal system, courts and police also have until recently treated domestic violence as unimportant — not a real crime. So men get away with it and women are frightened to complain. Nearly half of all murders of women are committed by their partners. There have been improvements in some areas where women are gaining equality — in education, some areas of employment and promotion — as well as legal equality.

To answer the question we would need to say the picture is mixed. In some areas men still have more power and control than women, in other areas women are becoming more equal. There still remain many areas where women need to fight for justice but most younger women have higher expectations for themselves than their mothers and grandmothers had in the past. Another point is that many women gain significant satisfaction from their roles as wives and mothers. Some households are moving towards more joint conjugal roles, and where both partners work full time a comfortable lifestyle can be achieved. However, overall research points to the fact that generally in marriage, the family and the wider society, women are at a disadvantage to men.

There is recognition here that there have been only limited moves towards greater equality between men and women, and this gains marks for evaluation. The term patriarchy is used and explained and provides a good context for the section. The paragraph sums up some key points and is well related to the question. Quite good evaluation skills are displayed. This answer would gain 18 out of 24 marks. Evaluation needs to be more thorough and focused, and theory used more strategically, to gain full marks. There should be a clear rationale in the organisation of the material, leading to a distinct conclusion.

Overall mark: 50/60

Changes in the family and the contribution of feminism

Read Items 2A and 2B and answer parts (a) to (e) that follow.

Item 2A

There have been unprecedented changes in family life over recent years. Women are having fewer children, more couples are deciding to remain child-free, there has been an increase in single-person households, fewer marriages are taking place, and one in four children lives in a lone-parent family. On the surface it would appear that there is evidence of a crisis in the institution of marriage and family life.

However, the evidence needs to be interpreted carefully. For example, the decline in marriage has much to do with couples delaying marriage rather than never marrying at all. There are also ethnic variations, for example some women of Pakistani and South Asian heritage marry relatively young. Commentators point out that by the age of 40, 95% of women and 91% of men have married (Bernardes 1997). Although the divorce rate rose sharply after 1969 and remains high, in 2005 there was an 8% fall in the number of people divorcing. It must also be remembered that the reason many people divorce is in order to remarry. So the divorce rate may be an expression of dissatisfaction with a particular partner rather than dissatisfaction with being married.

Item 2B

Feminists such as Ann Oakley have made major contributions to the ways sociologists study the family. Pre-feminism, women's role was seen to be predominantly the wife and mother in the family and men's role was as bread-winner, and much research accepted this pattern as given or the norm. Feminists have highlighted the inequalities and different perceptions men and women have of their roles in the family. They have also provided an analysis of the economic contribution of women's domestic labour to society. Recently, some feminist perspectives have focused on the variety of experiences of women in the family, as well as the improvements there have been in family life for many women. Other feminists have challenged the view that 'the family' exists as a single institution, while others have looked at the role of social policy as a support for conventional family structure.

(a) **Explain what is meant by the term 'divorce rate'.** (2 marks)

(b) **Explain the difference between a family that is child-free and one that is childless (Item 2A).** (4 marks)

(c) Suggest *three* reasons for the increase in the divorce rate between 1971 and 2005 (Item 2A). (6 marks)

(d) Examine some of the ways in which it could be argued that family life has improved for women since the 1950s. (24 marks)

(e) Using material from Item 2B and elsewhere, assess the contribution of feminist perspectives to the study of the family. (24 marks)

■ ■ ■

Answer to question 2: grade-C candidate

(a) The divorce rate is the number of marriages legally ended every year.

> 🖉 When you see the word 'rate' in a question such as this, remember that a 'rate' will refer to something that is being measured against something else. In this case, the divorce rate is usually calculated as the number of people divorcing per year per 1,000 of the number of married people, or sometimes the number of divorces in a given year per 1,000 marriages. No marks were given for this answer.

(b) The term 'child-free' means deliberately deciding not to have children, i.e. a positive decision. The term 'childless' implies that a couple want children and cannot have them for some reason.

> 🖉 Four marks were given for this answer.

(c) Women are now more likely to divorce their husbands if they are unhappy. The 1969 Divorce Reform Act (in force in 1971) gave them the right to do this if they could show that the marriage had broken down. Marriages last longer now because of longer life expectancy and are therefore more likely to end in divorce not death. Women are now less financially and emotionally dependent on men, so feel more confident about ending a marriage and living alone.

> 🖉 Three clear reasons are given and expanded on — 6 marks.

(d) Women's lives have improved enormously in the family in recent times. Women have many labour-saving devices in the home, such as dishwashers, washing machines, microwaves, fridge-freezers so that they don't have to spend so long on housework now. In the past women would have had to shop every day, cook meals from scratch and then wash up by hand. Men now take a much more active role in housework and childcare and take some of the pressure off women. The term 'New Man' has been used to describe these changes whereby there is no stigma attached to men doing jobs that previously were considered to be women's work.

> 🖉 These are potentially relevant points but are made in a somewhat commonsensical manner rather than showing sociological understanding. No supporting evidence is provided here for the points about the time spent on housework or childcare by the New Man.

Women have become more independent from men in the last 50 years and usually go out to work now even if they have children. This means that they are more likely to make financial contributions to the household and therefore are more involved in decisions about how money is spent than in the past. Girls now have more opportunities when they leave school and have higher expectations of having a happy and fulfilling family life. Marriage is seen as an equal partnership today whereas in the past it might just have been an economic contract. Conjugal roles are more likely to be joint now with men sharing more domestic tasks. Also women have equal rights with men in law and in the family.

✍ An important point about changing girls'/women's expectations of their marriages and family lives is made but no evidence is offered to underpin the argument. There was an opportunity to include some feminist research here.

Women have fewer children today, two or three is the average size of family, whereas in the past women had many children because they had no reliable contraception. This has given women more freedom and time to devote to their children. They can also go back to work earlier. So overall women's family life has changed a lot over the last 50 years but perhaps not as much as might be expected. However, feminists have shown that things have not improved for all women, some suffer domestic violence and others still do the majority of domestic work in the home as well as paid work outside the home.

✍ **The candidate has made some good points, although their relevance to the question could have been more explicit. There is a lack of evidence from research studies and an 'argument' is not developed. The main problem with this answer is the limited amount of evaluation or opposing argument about how changes do not affect all women and/or that some of the 'improvements', such as men doing more housework, have been overstated and are not supported by the evidence. Hence, this essay gains the majority of its marks for knowledge and understanding. Overall, this answer would score 12 out of 24 marks.**

(e) The first perspective I am going to look at is the liberal feminist perspective on the family. Liberal feminists believe that it is possible to bring about equality between men and women through making legal and social changes in our current society. There is no need for radical, violent or revolutionary change as put forward by other perspectives. Their approach pushes for working through the legal structures of society in order to improve women's lives. The Equal Pay Act and the Sex Discrimination Act of 1970 are examples of legal ways to outlaw discrimination on the basis of sex. Employers are no longer allowed to employ men over women or to pay them less for doing the same job. Women now have the right to maternity leave and pay so that they can go back to work after having a baby. It is also illegal to sack a pregnant woman. In addition, power relations between partners in the family have become more equal, for example more men do housework and childcare now. Because most women now work, there is said to be more mutual support for spouses in family life. Wilmott and Young's study in 1975 found the beginnings of a symmetrical family and they argued that this would filter down to the rest of society in time. Tony Blair introduced many more female candidates to stand for parliament to try to increase the number of women MPs in 1997, this worked to some extent so there is now more representation of women in parliament where the laws are made.

> This is a reasonably good opening paragraph that gets right to the point and gives a range of examples to illustrate the liberal feminist perspective. The language is not always as clear as it might be.

However, other feminists have disputed the liberal feminist claims. They say that despite changes in the law women still face discrimination at work and often have to fight for equal pay through industrial tribunals. Many cases have been highlighted and even local councils have been proven to discriminate against female employees such as dinner ladies. Also women still earn on average only about three-quarters of male earnings and men still seem to get the top jobs. Although evidence shows that many women are moving into management there is a 'glass ceiling' which seems to prevent them from getting right to the top. Women also seem to lose out when they have children and are overlooked for promotion after they become mothers.

> Some evaluation of the liberal feminist perspective is introduced here, showing an awareness of the limitations of the approach. The term 'other feminists' is used, rather than specifying which ones. However, use of evidence adds strength to the answer.

Another area that shows women's subordinate position is domestic violence in the home. The figures show clearly that a large proportion of women, according to Dobash and Dobash, are the victims of violence by men. Some women each year are killed by their partners. Other research by Oakley has found that despite claims about equality in the home women still carry the burden of housework and childcare as well as working outside the home. Patriarchal attitudes are still prevalent in society particularly some areas of the media.

> **The candidate clearly ran out of time. This is quite a common feature of some A-level answers, and it shows the importance of keeping a check on your timing. Note, too, that only one feminist perspective is discussed, while the question clearly expects more than one perspective to be identified. The research evidence offered is rather dated, particularly that by Oakley. Therefore, the question would only gain 11 out of 24 marks.**

Overall mark: 33/60

Tip Keep your eye on the time throughout the exam. There is always a clock in the room if you do not have your own watch.

■ ■ ■

Answer to question 2: grade-A candidate

(a) The divorce rate is the number of legally granted terminations of marriage in a given year per 1,000 married couples.

> 🖉 This is a correct answer: the correct definition of 'divorce rate' is given — 2 marks.

(b) The term 'childless' usually implies that a couple want children but are unable to have them for a medical reason. There is sometimes a certain negative implication to the term. 'Child-free' has been used by women to counter the view that not having any children is negative. Child-free means making a deliberate and positive choice not to have children.

> 🖉 This is a clearly expressed explanation of the difference between the two terms — 4 marks.

(c) One reason for the increase in divorce is that the laws have changed to enable more couples to end their marriages legally, the main one being the Divorce Reform Act which became law in 1971. The second reason is that there is no stigma attached to being divorced any more especially for women. The third reason is that people have higher expectations of marriage and romantic love these days and when marriage doesn't live up to these expectations divorce is more likely.

> 🖉 Here are three clear reasons. Each one is identified in a separate sentence (though bullet points would have been acceptable), each of which reads well and is clearly expressed — 6 marks. Other reasons could be increasing life expectancy, decline in the power of religious belief and the church, and increasing independence of women.

(d) Women's lives have improved in the postwar period. One aspect relates to child-bearing. Women are in better health, partly because they have fewer children. In the past contraception was unreliable and women often had many children. Each pregnancy increases risks for women's health, particularly if the woman is over 40. The fertility rate has been falling for many years and reached an all-time low in 2001 when it was 1·63. However, in 2006 there was a mini-boom, according to national government statistics, when the ratio increased to 1.87. There is now also antenatal care for all women and the maternal mortality rate is low, this indicates a good general level of health for women. Having only two or three children means that women don't have to work as hard to care for them as they did with large numbers of children in the past. Women are now in more control over their fertility. There is reliable contraception and the morning-after pill and legal abortion if there is a need. Most women go out to work now as well as having children. All of these factors have improved family life for women.

> 🖉 This is a generally good opening paragraph which relates well and clearly to the question. The point about women going out to work needs further clarification to relate it to the question. The last sentence contextualises the previous points. It is

wise to go back and read the question again, noting that it states that it is improvements in 'family life' that you are being asked to examine.

Another area of family life that has improved for women are the laws relating to family life and behaviour. Husbands are no longer legally allowed to mistreat or abuse their wives. In the past men were unlikely to be prosecuted for rape, physical or mental abuse in marriage whereas now women can divorce their abusive husbands for these things. Women have protection from the law: a recent law prevents husbands from raping their wives. However, as the research from Dobash and Dobash shows, domestic violence is still a feature of some women's lives. Attitudes have changed to improve the status of women and they themselves have higher expectations of a happy family life. Women expect to be treated with respect. There is a general belief in equality between the sexes with women playing a central role in the decision-making and finances of the family.

It was once felt that women should do all the housework and childcare. Nowadays men help in the house. There is no longer a stigma which stops men doing housework or childcare. Some have argued that there are now joint conjugal roles. Young and Wilmott's research shows the family will become symmetrical with men and women sharing tasks. Men often want to take a full and active part in their children's upbringing and this has taken some of the burden off women. Their lives have improved because of this and marriage is now seen as more of a partnership. However, feminist research still shows that women take the major responsibility for housework and childcare. As Marxists argue this is for the benefit of capitalism and is a cheap way to produce and reproduce the next generation of workers. Feminists also doubt the sharing of domestic labour. Ann Oakley's 1970s research provided evidence of unequal conjugal roles especially after children are born, something backed up by other more recent research. Other feminists point to the patriarchal nature of the family.

Women now have the freedom to go to work if they want to unlike the immediate postwar years when they were expected to stay at home. They are no longer confined to the house looking after children. There has been the creation of labour-saving devices like washing machines, microwaves and vacuum cleaners which have reduced the amount of time women spend on housework. Fridges make storing food for longer periods possible so that shopping only takes place once a week whereas before it had to be done every day.

🖉 Many relevant points are made in these paragraphs. Some key sociological research is used to back up comments. There is also evidence of evaluation with counter-arguments about the improvements to women's lives in the family.

Women now have equality in education, their expectations for their own lives and prospects are higher. They expect to have careers and they expect to have happy family lives too. Although feminists have mixed views on the changing role of women and the changes that have taken place in the family, they all agree that the women's liberation movement has had an influence on life patterns for women.

Improved contraceptives, working outside the home, as well as the high divorce rate, the increase in cohabitation and later marriage have all had an impact on women and show that women are now more in control of their lives especially in the family.

Postmodernists would contribute to this discussion by pointing out that women cannot be treated as an homogeneous group, they come from different class and ethnic backgrounds, they have different identities and a range of different experiences depending upon their circumstances. Not all the improvements I have discussed apply to all women. Some women still suffer abuse and lack of power in the family. Others cannot find work which is sufficiently highly paid to help them achieve independence.

So, the picture is mixed. While there have been improvements for women in the family, they do not apply to all women across the board. It must be recognised that women are a diverse, heterogeneous group, which will impact upon their experience of family life.

> 🖉 **Twenty out of 24 marks were given for this section. To gain additional marks, the candidate could have drawn together some of the key factors that have created more independence for women — such as earning their own wages, higher expectations of marriage alongside improved control over their fertility. The piece reads in a slightly disjointed way, which detracts from the discussion about the overall improvement in women's lives within the family. However, the final point about the postmodernist view shows a knowledge of current new debates and provides further evaluation.**

(e) Prior to the development of feminist perspectives in the 1960s when the Women's Liberation Movement (WLM) began, there was an assumption that all demands for equality applied to all women and that when equality was achieved it would be for all women, black, white, young, old, middle class, working class, working women, housewives. The focus of much of the movement was towards achieving equal rights at work for women in the belief that if women could achieve economic independence from men other forms of independence would follow. Key campaigns were around equal pay for equal work, an end to sex discrimination, free contraception and abortion, free childcare. When it was realised that the WLM was a mainly white, middle-class movement other aspects of women's experiences were understood to be just as important as, but different from, the original concerns of the WLM.

> 🖉 This opening paragraph provides a historical context to the development of different types of feminist perspective. It locates the origins of the Women's Liberation Movement (WLM) as being the focal point for campaigns for equality for women in society, out of which grew the various feminist perspectives we study in sociology today. The paragraph creates in the reader's mind a clear understanding of the background to contemporary feminism.

The first perspective I will assess is the Marxist feminist perspective. Marxist feminists accept the analysis that Karl Marx provided of a capitalist society. The fundamental point is that capitalism is based on the inequality between social classes. That inequality is based on the ownership of property of the two major classes in society — the bourgeoisie and the proletariat. The ruling class or bourgeoisie own the means of production, the working class or proletariat own their labour, which they sell to the bourgeoisie for a wage. All other forms of oppression and exploitation flow from the inequality and conflict between the ruling class and the working class. Women are seen to be doubly exploited under capitalism, by the ruling class and by men through an ideology created by capitalism which puts forward the view that because men are the main bread-winners in a capitalist society women are subordinate to men. Their main role is wife and mother, their role as worker is secondary and they are used as a reserve army of labour. So for Marxist feminists women's oppression is first by capitalism and then by men, they suffer double exploitation. The ideology of the nuclear family is also seen by Marxist feminists as a further means of oppression in that it is a 'private' sphere of life that is meant to represent a safe haven in a harsh world, when in reality it can be a dangerous place. The solution to women's oppression for Marxist feminists is a total revolutionary overthrow of the capitalist system of production and its replacement with a socialist society.

The problem with this analysis is that even in societies not based solely on capitalism and social class, such as China, the former Soviet Union and even native peoples such as Aborigines and First Nations people, women are still seen as second class. Men in these cultures wield the power and control. Women are seen as inferior to men and as of lower status. In China and India for example, baby girls are more likely to be orphaned or abandoned as male children are seen to be much more desirable. Hence, critics have argued that oppression is more to do with gender relations than social class, with men being the main agents of exploitation. This would be the view of the radical feminists. Liberal feminists would argue that even within a capitalist society it is possible to gain equality for women through changes in the law and changes in attitudes. They believe that the capitalist system can be adjusted to create a more egalitarian society, and there is evidence of this in the passing of the Equal Pay and Sex Discrimination Acts in the 1970s. Liberal feminists would also point out that women's lives have improved dramatically during the last 50 years in all areas — family, work, relationships etc.

🖉 The first paragraph of this section gives a detailed and accurate description of the Marxist feminist perspective. The candidate provides several areas of assessment of the Marxist feminist perspective. Other perspectives are used in the second paragraph to criticise the Marxist feminist view, showing good evaluation skills. This paragraph could also have looked at the different experiences of women, e.g. black women and racism, to illustrate the problem of using social class as the defining feature of inequality in society.

The second perspective I am going to consider is the radical feminists. Radical feminist analysis begins from the point that men are the main oppressors of women. Men and women are viewed as a 'sex-class', with men having all the power and control in society, exploiting and oppressing women in a variety of ways for their own benefit both physically and mentally. Men exploit women as housewives and mothers, men oppress women as workers by paying them less and forcing them into lower status jobs. Men even oppress women sexually and use the fear of rape as a form of control to keep women off the streets and more confined to their homes after dark. Writers such as Dale Spender also point out through their research how men dominate women in social situations and use language to maintain their powerful position. Patriarchy is a system of male domination present in all societies and all cultures, and Firestone believes that it is based on men's biology and physical strength, which is incorporated into social-isation of children in the nuclear family. Other feminists have criticised radical feminism for painting a completely negative picture of male/female relationships when for many women heterosexual relationships and family life are fulfilling. Radical feminism does not present a unified perspective on women's lives but ideas from a variety of viewpoints such as radical separatist lesbianism, which advocates liberation through separation from men, and revolutionary perspectives, which seek to overthrow the 'tyranny' of men. One of the main concerns is that radical feminism only ever represented a small minority of women and had little to say about the lives of most ordinary women. It has been the main cause of negativity about equal rights campaigners, who are labelled with the 'man-hater' stigma. Indeed the word feminism is often synonymous with 'anti-male'. Radical feminism is seen as just an attack on men and providing little sociological analysis of the nature of women's oppression or subordination.

This paragraph provides critical and evaluative comments about the radical feminist perspective but there is as yet no direct reference to Item 2B. This paragraph could have located the radical feminist perspective within the context of the postwar first phase of feminism and particularly a branch of the women's movement that emerged in the 1960s and 1970s, when more women were going to university and using their education to understand why women were unable to achieve success in many areas of social life, not least the world of work.

Postmodernists would argue that the main failure of traditional feminist perspect-ives has been the inability to explain and understand the experiences of all women. As mentioned in Item 2B there is a wide variety of experiences in women's lives. Women cannot be treated as an homogeneous group. They differ according to ethnicity, social class, age and a whole range of other factors which contribute to their identity. There are differences according to women's position in the global economy which feminism is only now beginning to analyse. It has also been interesting to note that even when women do achieve powerful positions in companies, government or education they do not necessarily act in the interests of women. Feminists have challenged the 'malestream' perspective of traditional sociology and put the consideration of issues to do with gender at the centre of the debate.

Finally, as Item 2B points out, some feminists draw attention to the fact that 'the' family does not exist. There are many different types of family structure, and women's experiences within them can be quite different. The view that policies only support the conventional family could also be challenged, as there are state benefits for lone parents, and lesbian and gay couples have also been allowed to adopt children.

This essay would achieve 20 marks out of 24. It shows sufficient depth and detail and is evaluative throughout. There is a good understanding of recent developments in feminism through the postmodernist discussion. There is some reference to the Item in the last two paragraphs; full marks could have been gained if the Item had been referred to earlier.

Overall mark: 52/60

Task Write down a list of key concepts associated with feminist perspectives.

Childhood, social policy and perspectives on the family

Read Items 2A and 2B below and answer parts (a) to (e) that follow.

Item 2A

In modern industrial society the period we know as childhood is marked out by a set of cultural practices that are separate from adulthood. It is often assumed that childhood is a natural state but in fact it is largely a social construction. It is only from about the seventeenth century in Western societies that childhood has been seen as a separate life-stage; before this, children were integrated into the adult world from about the age of four or five. In other words, in the past once children moved beyond the physical dependence stage they were regarded by society as adults. Medieval paintings of children show them dressed as adults, participating in an adult life. However, childhood has increasingly been seen as a distinct state, and social policies such as laws preventing children from working have further enforced 'age patriarchy' and the enforced segregation of children.

Item 2B

Social policies either directly or indirectly have assumed that the family should take a particular form and play a particular role in society. This is evident in the laws passed that affect the roles of women and children. Some feminists have argued that many such laws have patriarchal power, which, although not as blatant as in the past, when men were permitted by law to use physical violence against women and children, nevertheless still permeates family roles and structures. Unequal power relationships therefore still exist between men and women, and between adults and children. However, some sociologists would argue that gendered roles within the family and clear differences in power relationships are, in fact, beneficial both for individuals and for society as a whole.

(a) Explain what is meant by 'age patriarchy'. (2 marks)
(b) Identify *two* ways in which children nowadays are segregated from adult society. (4 marks)
(c) Identify *three* aspects of childhood that show how childhood is socially constructed. (6 marks)
(d) Examine some of the ways in which social policies can affect families. (24 marks)

3

(e) Using material from the Items and elsewhere, outline and assess two sociological perspectives on the family. (24 marks)

■ ■ ■

Answer to question 3: grade-C candidate

(a) Age patriarchy means control over children.

> *⌨* There is not enough detail to get the marks. The answer would need to refer to adult power/control over the lives of children.

(b) By having earlier bedtimes than adults. Not being in the adult world of work or play.

> *⌨* This is not written in sentence form and that detracts from the sense and meaning of the points being made. Bullet-point answers are acceptable in this type of question, but it is important that the meaning is made quite clear. There is some notion of the separation of adults and children, particularly in the second part, so this answer would gain 2 out of 4 marks.

(c) Children are protected from aspects of the adult world such as sex and death. Children have laws especially for them, like having to go to school.

> *⌨* There is insufficient detail for full marks, and only two aspects of childhood have been identified, rather than the three that were asked for. There is little here to show that the student really understands the meaning of 'social construction'. Two marks are awarded, one for each of the two points made. To gain the further marks available, a third aspect of childhood should have been identified, and the notion of 'social construction' should have been made explicit by giving more detail, for example full-time education extends the period of dependency.

(d) There have been lots of laws passed which affect families. The law allows abortion and contraception as well as IVF. Therefore families can decide how many children to have and when to have them. The structure of the family is affected by social policies and welfare payments such as child benefit. If someone is caring for an elderly or sick member of the family they can claim attendance allowance which provides financial help. There is divorce and people cohabit with each other now. Marriage is also popular.

> *⌨* This opening paragraph is a list of possible laws/policies/benefits that may affect the family, but the candidate has not gone on to show how the material is relevant to the question. The material has not been applied and therefore the question is not being answered explicitly at this point. However, some knowledge of social policies is evident.

Feminists have said that the policies and laws on the family are patriarchal and therefore benefit men. Until recently only women could get maternity leave when they had a baby. Only women are paid child benefit. This means that the government believes women should be the main child-carers. Marxists would agree with feminists and say that capitalism supports the nuclear family as the best form of family that benefits capitalism. The New Right would disagree with giving benefits to single mothers and always wants benefits for the nuclear family — mother, father and children. Charles Murray believes that only the nuclear family should be supported through social policies and welfare benefits. They should not be paid to people who do not conform to society's values, like teenage mothers, who he sees as a threat to the fabric of our society.

🖉 There is evidence here of some theoretical understanding and analysis. However, it is expressed briefly. To gain more marks there would have to be elaboration of the points to show how the perspectives can be used to demonstrate the impact of social policy and law on the family.

The New Right is also against gay couples even though the law has changed and gay couples can have a civil partnership and equality with non-gays in the law. The family has many functions, like raising children, socialisation, care for members, providing a home, emotional support, and social policies support these functions. Also these functions can be done by different sorts of families.

🖉 **This answer would achieve 10 marks as it shows some sociological knowledge but is limited in application, interpretation, analysis and evaluation skills. There is little structure and coherence to the piece, which is another reason why it falls into the lower mark band. The candidate never really gets to grips with answering the question, but there are some indications that there is an understanding of perspectives.**

(e) The first perspective I am going to look at is the functionalist perspective on the family. The nuclear family is seen as the family that best fits the needs of industrial societies. Functionalists believe the nuclear family serves particular purposes in society, the socialisation of children and the expression of adults' role, men as breadwinners and women as wives and mothers. This is a stereotypical idea as today most women also work outside the home. Children are taught the norms and values of society and how they should behave. They are taught their future adult roles and encouraged to find work roles. The functionalists think the family is a positive institution for individuals and for society. The second perspective is the Marxist perspective which views the nuclear family in a negative way. Marxists see the family as a product of capitalism which supports a capitalist ideology through socialisation of the young. The role given to men and women in the family creates inequality and oppression, with men having the power. Engels believed that the family is tied to the needs of the economy and therefore serves the interests of the ruling class. For Engels the nuclear family produces the next generation of workers for the capitalists. Zaretsky, a more recent Marxist writer, also points out that the family can act as a 'safety net' in a harsh and oppressive world. It provides the emotional support for its members so there can be something positive in family life too.

e This answer is brief for a 24-mark question. While it is, of course, the quality rather than the quantity of what is written that gains marks, short answers are unlikely to cover sufficient ground to get into the higher mark bands. This answer does not really address both aspects of the question and no reference is made to the Items. There are some brief evaluative comments. By the juxtaposition of the two perspectives outlined, the candidate shows that functionalists have a positive view of the nuclear family and Marxists a negative one. There is no evidence, however, of a thorough assessment of each perspective and the arguments that could be used to show the strengths and weaknesses of these views. However, the descriptions that are put forward are quite accurate and show some understanding of basic tenets of each. There is also some awareness of different writers linked to the Marxist perspective. This candidate scores marks based mainly on knowledge and understanding skills rather than interpretation, analysis or evaluation. This answer would score 10 marks out of 24.

Overall mark: 24/60

Task Write down in note form some points related to the question that would enable the candidate to achieve higher marks:

- Write a list of the key points that cover all the important aspects of each perspective.
- What studies could you use?
- How could you incorporate information from the **Items** to help you in your answer?
- Which sources of information or writers from '**elsewhere**' could you use?
- Write a list of points that show you can **evaluate** or **assess** the perspectives you have chosen to write about.
- Consider the way the 'family' is defined by each perspective.

■ ■ ■

Answer to question 3: grade-A candidate

(a) Age patriarchy means that adults, probably more often men, have control over children's lives. This can be at an individual level, in the home, as well as at a societal level, e.g. laws controlling aspects of children's lives and behaviour.

e The explanation is full, clear and correct — 2 marks.

(b) One way children are segregated from adults is that by law they have to go to school between the ages of 5 and 16. A second way that children are separated from adults is by not being allowed to go to work on a full-time basis until they are 16.

e Two clear examples of the segregation of children from adults — 4 marks.

(c) Childhood is socially constructed in that we believe children are vulnerable and should be protected and supervised until they are able to look after themselves. Second, children are socialised into the norms and values of society as well as being taught 'right and wrong' by adults. The law says that they are not legally responsible for their actions below a certain age. Third, children are completely dependent on adults and live in a 'children's world' where they are dressed as children, play as children and have toys which are especially for children.

🖉 Three clear ways in which childhood is constructed; the answer is laid out and expressed well — 6 marks.

(d) Social policies are laws which bring about changes in particular areas of social life like the family. There have been many social policies which have been introduced to 'support' and strengthen the family both by Conservative and Labour governments, such as child benefit, attendance allowance, maternity leave and pay, and recently paternity leave. But many policies have assumed that the family is a particular type — the nuclear family with mother, father and children living together under the same roof. The New Right policies of the Thatcher governments were blatantly anti-single parents, treating them as deviant, and there was a reduction in benefits to lone mothers. Tax privileges were given to married couples but not co-habiting couples. John Major tried to introduce 'back to basics' and 'family values' to social policy initiatives which again attacked single, fatherless families as creating an undisciplined underclass and were based on the ideas of Charles Murray. However, underlying New Right policy was a strongly patriarchal view that a woman's rightful place in the family was as a child-bearer and carer, and a traditional nuclear family. 'Care in the community' has been seen by feminists as an attempt to create care of the elderly and sick by women in the home. Much welfare provision has ideological assumptions underpinning it which seek to restrict women and nuclear families to their traditional role. Freedom from state control in the 1980s was seen as increasingly leaving the rearing of children and the care of the elderly and sick to the domain of the family. The Conservatives also set up the Child Support Agency to chase absent fathers and make them pay for the upbringing of their children — to force them to take responsibility as member of a family.

🖉 This opening shows an understanding of the New Right ideology and its link to policy development of that period. The ideological and political aspects of social policy are explained well.

The image of the family under New Labour thinking was not much different. In the late 1990s New Labour produced their 'Supporting Families' green paper. This reiterated the idea that the 'best' family was a nuclear family with moral responsibility for the stability of society. Single parents are seen as deviant and dysfunctional for the individual and society. Marriage and family life are seen as crucial for the proper upbringing of children. New Labour has set up the Sure Start scheme whereby parents can get support and help with parenting skills as well as beginning to educate and socialise children properly for their entry into school. This policy has been targeted at the poor in order to try to bring their family lives up to the 'required standard' of the traditional nuclear family.

This paragraph encapsulates the New Left views on social policy and the family, linking them clearly to the New Right.

Feminists have always been critical of social policy and the family because of the restrictive ideological views about what constitutes a family and what roles should be played in the family. Rather than providing more freedom for women many social policies, they argue, restrict women to their traditional roles as wives, mothers and carers. The ideological standpoint that childcare is a job for mothers is one that feminists take particular issue with since it sums up the whole nature of a patriarchal society where men have power and economic control. Social policies affecting the family have changed considerably since the original Beveridge plan of the 1940s, which was to fight a war on poverty. The system of universal benefits through a contributory national insurance scheme to provide free education and healthcare to all members of society has been overtaken with means-tested benefits designed to weed out those who do not meet the 'traditional' standards.

Hence, social policies have a direct impact upon families of all types but their effect cannot be seen as separate from the ideological underpinning of the policy makers. Both Labour and Conservative governments have produced social policies which can be shown to favour traditional marriage and the nuclear family. All other living arrangements and especially single-parent fatherless families have been vilified. From the setting up of the Child Support Agency to the Children's Act and Supporting Families, social policies have been ideological in nature. The Marxists therefore believe that social policies have the main effect of supporting the capitalist system and creating a form of family most suited to its needs.

This answer shows quite strong theoretical understanding of the issues concerning social policy and the family. There is substantial evaluation throughout the answer, which scores 20 out of 24 marks. More could have been said about the ways in which social policies affect families — these policies do not always bring about the expected or desired outcomes, for example, the number of lone-parent families has continued to increase despite the negative social policies mentioned in the answer, and the number of teenage mothers has gone up.

(e) Given that the family in some form is a universal institution in society, it is no surprise that different groups of sociologists have devoted considerable time to studying and analysing it. However, they often disagree about its function and importance for society.

This is a good, brief introduction which sets the scene for the subsequent discussion.

The Marxist perspective on the family is critical of the form the family takes under capitalism. Marxists argue that the nuclear family has been created to fulfil the needs of a capitalist system of economic production. Men are seen as the bread-winners and women are seen as the wives and mothers or workers if needed. The system perpetuates itself through socialisation of the young and patriarchal ideology and hegemony which teaches children and adults that these roles are natural. Other institutions in society such as the education system, the mass media, religion etc. also perpetuate the ideology of familism. Engels argued that the need for monogamy only emerged when the ownership of private property came about and the desire to pass on wealth to one's offspring became desirable. He also argued that industrialisation led to the enslavement of women as domestic servants excluded from production and earning power. He claimed that men represented the bourgeoisie and women the proletariat in the capitalist family. Zaretsky in 1976, although a Marxist, argued that the family provides an illusion of security and emotional support against the harsh, oppressive world of capitalism. More recently writers have been influenced by the work of Foucault and looked at the family as a form of body surveillance. This form of social control is becoming an increasingly important aspect of family life whereby parental discipline and authority are brought to bear on family members through the day-to-day activities which take place behind the closed doors of the family home.

🖉 This paragraph sums up the main tenets of Marxism, using the key concept of ideology. Also, the candidate links in the important point about the form the family takes being dependent upon the capitalist system of production.

However, there have been many criticisms of the Marxist perspective. Its macro approach, which sees society as a whole entity, cannot provide an appropriate analysis that takes account of the variety and diversity of family life in modern society. There are a range of different family types and it could be argued that some do not directly serve the needs of capitalism. No account is taken or analysis provided of the meaning that individuals give to their experience of family life. There is also an ethnocentric aspect of the Marxist perspective, and other versions of the family based on ethnicity, race or religion are ignored. Class is seen as the determining characteristic of all aspects of family life but other dimensions such as gender could provide a different analysis. Postmodernist writers take issue with such metanarratives as Marxism because they cannot account for the diversity of family life.

🖉 Some good evaluative points are made which show an understanding of some of the limitations of the Marxist perspective on the family.

The second perspective I will outline is the functionalist perspective on the family. Functionalism, like Marxism, is also a system or macro perspective which sees society as a whole and the family as an aspect of that whole. Functionalists believe that the family evolves to meet individual and societal needs. Fletcher pointed out that the modern nuclear family emerged from the industrial revolution when there was a need for geographical mobility to find employment. Therefore, functions that were previously performed by the family have been taken over by other agencies such as the welfare state and the education system. This was followed, according to Murdock, by a decline in the functions performed by the family to four basic ones — sexual, reproductive, economic and educational. The family became more specialised in the functions it performed as the state took over more and more functions. Talcott Parsons talks of the two basic and irreducible functions of the nuclear family in industrial society — socialisation of the young and the stabilisation of adult personalities. Parsons suggests that there is a natural or biological division of labour within the nuclear family — the husband is the breadwinner and the wife supports the emotional needs of the husband and cares for the children.

> The candidate provides a clear outline of some of the main traditional functionalist writers on the family and explains the key concepts well. Functionalism is contextualised well as a 'whole-society' perspective, which makes the following material more relevant.

Functionalism has been heavily criticised in sociology for many years and much of the theory has been rejected. However, it has reappeared in recent years in the guise of New Right and New Left socio-political perspectives, which have been fundamental to much government analysis and policy. Feminists in particular take issue with the harmonious, idealistic view such perspectives put forward. They point to the incontrovertible evidence of many negative aspects of family life — marital breakdown, domestic violence and child abuse. Feminists would also criticise the view that the division of labour in the family is natural and point to many societies where male and female roles are much more fluid, certainly not universal. There are many different types of family in modern society, whereas the functionalist merely assumes the dominance of the nuclear family. Marxist feminists would particularly point to the class nature of society and the effects of this on the ideology of the family. It is broadly accepted that functionalism is based on an idealistic image of the middle-class all-American family. It is therefore quite limited, even on a macro scale, in providing a thorough analysis of the nature of the family in modern society. Postmodernists would argue that the many different types of family that now exist are a reflection of how society has changed. Individuals develop 'families' that suit their needs and experiences. In conclusion, a 'one-size-fits-all' family no longer exists, if indeed it ever did.

> **There is evaluation of the Marxist and functionalist perspectives on the family in this answer, with reference to both feminism and postmodernism in the last paragraph. Some of the points would benefit from further elaboration but there is a feeling that the candidate is running out of time and rushing the closing section of the answer. Always try to make sure you leave enough time to complete your work. Overall, this candidate displays good knowledge, analysis and evaluation, and produces an answer that remains focused on the question throughout,**

gaining 22 out of 24 marks. The structure of the answer is generally logical and coherent.

Overall mark: 54/60

Task Take three or four points that were made in the last section of this answer and write an additional sentence to develop each point in order to score more evaluation marks.

Industrialisation and changes in the functions of the family; the postmodern view of the family

Read Items 2A and 2B and answer parts (a) to (e) that follow.

Item 2A

The dominant perspective in the sociology of the family in the past was functionalism. Parsons' view was that industrialisation had led to the development of the nuclear family to take the place of the extended family that had existed in pre-industrial society. He argued that the nuclear family was a good 'fit' for the industrial economy, providing a variety of functions that fulfilled the needs of both the individual and society. These functions are primary socialisation, preparation of young people for their working lives, socially condoned satisfaction of sexual needs, the stabilisation of adult personalities and a division of labour in the family along natural lines. Functionalists also believe that the nuclear family provides the necessary security and emotional support needed in an industrial society, where life can be harsh and stressful. The modern nuclear family can also be geographically mobile and free from kinship obligations, which enables the existence of an independent household structure.

Item 2B

Postmodernists dispute much of what the grand theories have to say about the family in sociology, taking particular exception to the functionalist and Marxist perspectives. According to the postmodern view, the family is a diverse, flexible arrangement with fluid and changing relationships. 'Family' means different things to different people, and individuals can make choices regarding the type of family to belong to, depending upon their needs and desires at any particular time in their life. Same-sex civil relationships, serial monogamy, lone parents, child-free families and singleton households are all aspects of the dynamic and changing family environment in the twenty-first century.

(a) **Explain what is meant by 'primary socialisation' (Item 2A).** (2 marks)

(b) **Suggest *two* differences between an extended and a nuclear family.** (4 marks)

(c) **Give *three* examples of how the nuclear family could be said to 'fit' the needs of industrial society.** (6 marks)

(d) Examine the evidence for the view that industrialisation brought about the change from an extended to a nuclear family structure. (24 marks)

(e) Using material from the Items and elsewhere, assess the reasons given by sociologists for the increasing diversity of family and household structure in the twenty-first century. (24 marks)

■ ■ ■

Answer to question 4: grade-A candidate

(a) Primary socialisation means the teaching of the norms and values of society to children when they are young, e.g. in the family.

> ☑ This is correct, it covers both elements — the family is the primary agent or institution to socialise children, and socialisation is indeed the teaching of norms and values — 2 marks.

(b) The extended family contains wider kin like grandparents or aunts and uncles either living together or nearby, whereas the nuclear family has just parents and children. A second difference is that an extended family can call on other family members for support like childcare, whereas the nuclear family lives by itself and is often isolated from kin.

> ☑ This achieves 4 marks as there are two clear differences. Other differences could include generational differences — vertical/horizontal — and the type of family — linked to agricultural or industrial society.

(c) The nuclear family fits the needs of industrial society by being able to move around to find work, by socialising children to go to school and work and having the right values to function in society and, third, by making sure adults understand their roles: fathers work outside the home, mothers provide childcare inside the home.

> ☑ This is a concise and clear answer. There are three examples of the 'fit' — geographical mobility, socialisation of the young, adult roles. However, it might have been even clearer for the examiner had the examples been numbered or laid out as bullet points — 6 marks.

> **Tip** Where a question asks for a specific number of examples, ensure your answer contains a clear separation of the points.

(d) Sociologists have discussed the idea that industrialisation was the main catalyst for changing the family from an extended to a nuclear structure. One argument is that the move away from agriculture to manufacturing industries in the towns and cities meant that the nuclear family had to split from the extended family members to move geographically to find work in the new centres of production. As Fletcher has argued, the extended families had lived and worked together on the land in agriculture and cottage industries before the growth of the industrial economy as a multi-functional unit. However, how evidence is interpreted depends upon how

question

the term 'extended family' is defined. If an extended family means living together or seeing each other every day face-to-face, then it has probably declined. If we mean keeping in contact with our grandparents, aunts, uncles and cousins, then extended kin connections are still important to many of us in industrial society.

 This is a focused and relevant opening paragraph that sets the scene for the essay. It mentions a main argument, geographical mobility, which has been put forward for the change from extended to nuclear families. The candidate also highlights the important fact that how we define an institution in society will affect our conclusions about its existence or change.

The view about the change from extended to nuclear is held by the functionalist and, to some extent, Marxist perspectives, both of which tie in the needs of the economy to the formations of other structures in society, like the family. However, there is evidence from ethnic minorities like Asian and Cypriot families that they have maintained an extended family structure in industrial societies. Even where family members don't live together they keep in constant contact and visit each other regularly as well as being a source of financial and emotional support. There is also evidence that working-class families tend to have contact with wider kin for support, in mining communities for example. Also, Young and Willmott found the existence of the extended family among the working class in the East End of London in the 1950s. However, this study is quite old and there has been considerable population movement out of London to the suburbs and the breakup of the extended family to a modified extended structure. Wilmott's more recent study in the 1980s in north London suggested that if we look at the contacts that relatives have with each other then a type of extended family is in existence today. He found that more than half of the people in his survey had regular and frequent contact with their wider kin. More recently in the 1990s Fiona Devine revisited the Luton car workers study done previously by Goldthorpe and Lockwood in the 1950s and found that extended kinship contact was evident and that the 'privatised' family is over-exaggerated. Finch and Mason also found that families in Manchester relied heavily upon their kin for help, support and advice. Help with childcare is a particular feature of family life in modern society because many mothers also go out to work and childcare is expensive. It is not possible, therefore, to say categorically that industrialisation brought about a nuclear family structure.

 This paragraph discusses appropriate perspectives and gives evidence from sociological research, with sociologists being identified accurately. Application, analysis and evaluation skills are in evidence.

Other evidence from Anderson, who looked at parish records in Preston, a northern industrial town, showed that families in the pre-industrial age contained on average four family members, i.e. a nuclear family structure existed. This was because there were high death rates and infant mortality rates. Parish records, however, may not be accurate as they were only collected by the local vicar and there was no law to force people to tell him about family changes. Laslett also found the existence of the extended family in modern industrial society and suggested that in the early days of the industrial revolution there was a greater need for extended kin to help in times of trouble. No unemployment benefit or other social benefits existed in those times and you needed to rely on your family to support you if you lost your job or were ill and not able to work. This is why children also needed to be sent out to work. This shows that industrialisation at least for a time led to the growth of the extended family rather than its decline.

e This paragraph shows some notion of the validity of methods used in Anderson's study. The two writers are identified accurately as relevant to the argument.

A further functionalist argument about the change from extended to nuclear families is that the family lost many of its functions in the industrial period, or functions become more specialised. For example, in pre-industrial agricultural society there was no education or healthcare system, so people relied on their families to learn skills or for medical care such as during childbirth. These functions have now been taken over by schools and the health service. People no longer need to rely on the family so much. Care homes look after old people so women can work. Children go to school.

All in all, the arguments and evidence are mixed about whether there is a direct link between industrialisation and the move to nuclear families. Marxists also believe that capitalism shapes the form the family takes so that the economy can benefit from women's domestic labour and childcare role and leave men free to work. The nuclear family is best suited to do this. How we define the extended family may have changed as we do not necessarily expect our extended kin to be living under the same roof but nevertheless we keep contact with them by e-mail, MySpace and Facebook these days. Perhaps we have 'virtual' families in the twenty-first century!

e **This is a good answer that maintains relevance throughout, identifies appropriate research and applies it to the question. There is evidence of good skills and evaluation. The candidate would score the maximum of 24 marks.**

(e) Sociologists have identified the many changes in society that have affected the structure of the family in recent years. Families are smaller as women are having fewer children or no children. There are more childless couples, single-person households and empty-nest families where children have grown up and left home. There is also the effect of increasing life expectancy so that many children these days know their great-grandparents and a large proportion of singleton households are older people, usually women. It is true to say that the high divorce rate has had an impact on the structure of the family too, increasing the number of single-parent households as well as increasing the number of blended or reconstituted families. Immigration to Britain has meant people with different cultures have brought their different types of family with them too. People from the Asian

subcontinent are more likely to maintain an extended family structure to provide support and help for each other.

e This is an impressive opening paragraph: it is relevant and focused on the question. Points are explained and a number of important concepts are introduced. Application skills are emerging from the beginning.

The most recent perspective to develop about the family is the postmodernist. Generally postmodernists believe that we have moved beyond the industrial age into an era dominated by the media and other forms of technology. As stated in Item 2B, postmodernists see the family in the post-industrial age as anything people want it to be. This means that we choose the kind of family relationships that most suit us. There is no right or wrong type of family, just a set of relationships that make sense to the individual at a particular time in their life. As individuals become freer to choose how they interpret reality, what they see as their family matches their needs at any one time. This means that there can be no all-encompassing family type in society which is better than another type. The previous sociological perspectives like functionalism, New Right and Marxism therefore no longer apply to the study of the family. The family structure is even more varied than in the past because society has changed and become more diverse and fluid.

e There is recognition here of how the theoretical framework can be applied to the question, showing a fairly accurate understanding of a postmodern theory applied to the family in the twenty-first century. The material is well linked to the question and contextualised. Appropriate reference has been made to the Item.

Another change which has led to diversity in family structure is the increase in ethnic minority groups who have migrated to the UK who have different sorts of families. South Asian families are usually close and rely heavily on the relatives and kin for support. Often these families are extended and live together or near each other. African Caribbean families represent a high proportion of lone parents, usually mothers, who sometimes marry after they have children. The high divorce rate has also led to an increase in single-parent households, albeit temporarily, an increase in blended or reconstituted families as people marry more than once during their lifetime. This process of serial monogamy means a growing number of children live with a step-parent and stepbrothers and stepsisters. As Item 2B states, this is evidence of increasing diversity in family life.

Attitudes to lone parents have changed and there is more acceptance of such arrangements. Also, people have children without being married and there is no stigma any more about cohabitation, which used to be called 'living in sin'. This reflects the declining influence of the church and religion in determining what is right or wrong in marriage and family life. Likewise there has been a relaxation of views about gay people and the law now prevents discrimination against homosexuals. There is evidence of gay couples having their own children or adopting children. We are more tolerant of these sorts of families today. So many people have experienced different types of families, and our attitudes and values about 'proper' family life have relaxed.

ℯ This is a wide-ranging paragraph with good points about the effect of the high divorce rate on family structure, the change in our attitudes, the rise in lone-parent families as well as families from minority ethnic groups and gay families.

Economic factors have played a part in the changing family structure too as more and more women go out to work. They do not want to have more than one or two children and this means smaller families and a decline in the fertility rate.

To conclude, it is probably true to say that there has always been variety and diversity in family life in the UK, not just in the twenty-first century. With most women now working outside the home, there has been a change in attitudes and values about different kinds of family life. Longer life expectancy and lower birth and fertility rates have all had their effect upon family structure. Lone-parent families, gay families, singletons, nuclear and extended or modified extended families, and reconstituted families are all the norm today.

ℯ **This concludes the essay and returns to the question to sum up the key points about diversity, although there is some repetition. Overall, this candidate has provided a well-written and relevant piece of work. There is evidence of good skills and evaluation as well as the application of some theory. The structure is coherent and logical and scores 19 out of 24 marks. To gain the other 5 marks, some of the points need to be elaborated to give a more detailed explanation, and postmodernism could have been used to underline the argument about increasing diversity in family organisation.**

Overall mark: 55/60

Question 5

Population statistics and change in the UK, the elderly and family life

Read Items 2A and 2B and answer parts (a) to (e) that follow.

Item 2A

The UK has an ageing population. This is a consequence of the ageing of the large numbers of children born after the Second World War and declining fertility rates and mortality rates. This has led to a decrease in the proportion of the population who are under 16 years of age and an increase in the number of people who are aged 65 and over.

Every year since 1901 (except 1976) there have been more births than deaths and therefore the population has grown. The UK population is projected to increase by 7.2 million over the period 2004 to 2031, though long-term projections are uncertain. In 2004 there were 3.33 people of working age for every person of state pensionable age.

Source: adapted from *National Statistics* online

Item 2B

In postmodern society the idea that age-specific experience is declining and that stages in the life course are becoming increasingly blurred has meant that there needs to be some reconsideration by sociologists of the role that age plays in social life. As Featherstone and Hepworth (1991) have suggested, the 'boundaries between age groups and generations have become increasingly blurred'. Children are becoming more adult-like, exposed to more and more aspects of what was once an adult-only world. Adults are becoming more child-like and enjoy many of the same leisure pursuits and pastimes as children, both in the home and through the global and electronic media.

(a) Explain what is meant by the 'natural increase' in population. (2 marks)

(b) Identify *two* possible effects on society of an ageing population. (4 marks)

(c) Suggest *three* reasons for the increase in life expectancy over the last 100 years. (6 marks)

(d) Examine some of the consequences for the family of changes in birth rates, death rates and family size since 1900. (24 marks)

(e) Using material from Item 2B and elsewhere, assess the extent to which 'boundaries between age groups and generations have become increasingly blurred' (Item 2B). (24 marks)

■ ■ ■

Answer to question 5: grade-A candidate

(a) There are more births than deaths in the population.

> ☑ This is correct — 2 marks. Note that the 'natural increase' does not include population growth due to the arrival of immigrants.

(b) One effect of an ageing population is that more grandparents are staying alive, so they can help the family with childcare. Another, this time negative, effect of an ageing population is that having more older people may be a burden on the health service.

> ☑ Two correct effects are identified — 4 marks. Other positive factors are: older people are staying on as part of the workforce, they are available to give advice and guidance to younger family members, they are more knowledgeable and have more life experience, they are more able to spend money on leisure time and holidays. Other negative factors are: they are a burden on the tax system and on the workforce, they have greater need for welfare benefits and take an unequal proportion of state benefits, using NHS resources more.

(c) (1) Improved knowledge of medicine and better healthcare, free after the introduction of the NHS.

(2) Women having fewer children, so less maternal mortality.

(3) Better working conditions — rules about health and safety at work protecting the workers.

> ☑ Three appropriate reasons are given — 6 marks. Note that in questions of this type it is acceptable to give note-type answers, rather than whole sentences. It is always a good idea to separate out your answers, so that the examiner can see easily that you have made the correct number of points.

(d) Changes in birth rates, death rates and family size have obvious consequences for society and for social policies. However, their effects are also felt at the level of individual families. One of the consequences of a declining birth rate is that families have fewer children and therefore invest much more in the upbringing of those children. Much more time, energy and money is spent upon the one, two or sometimes three children that most families now have. Many children are expected to gain a good education and stay on at school until the age of 18. They are therefore dependent on their parents for much longer than in the past.

> ☑ This paragraph makes the material used relevant to the question by identifying some of the consequences of a declining birth rate.

Since 1900 many laws have been passed to protect the rights of children and prevent them from being exploited. For example, they are not allowed to work before a certain age and they have to go to school by law. This makes them a cost to families and hence having a large number of children would mean much more expense for the parents as children no longer bring money into the family. With smaller families there is a higher likelihood of social mobility and affluence. Dual-income families can afford better housing and to buy consumer goods. With only two or three children in a family, parents can also spend more time with each one and their expectations of their children are often high. According to Berger and Berger, the family becomes child-centred. Parents want their children to achieve good jobs in their future lives and hence parents encourage and support their small families.

This section picks out some of the positive and negative consequences of dependency of children in smaller families and is therefore displaying evaluation skills. Good use is made of appropriate sociological concepts such as social mobility and affluence.

Another consequence of smaller families is the loss of functions of the family. As Fletcher has argued, the process of industrialisation has led to the decline in functions of the family with the state taking over education, socialisation, health and religious functions previously performed by the family. The family has now become more specialised in its functions as its size has reduced, according to functionalists. Talcott Parsons argues that the family now performs only two 'basic and irreducible functions', the socialisation of children and the stabilisation of adult personalities. This means the nuclear family teaches the young how to internalise the culture of society and provides a haven for adults to rest, relax and escape from the tensions of the world.

The increase in life expectancy as a result of falling death rates among adults also has consequences for the family in that there are more and more older people in families who may need caring for. This can be a burden on families, particularly if the elderly relatives become ill or infirm. Although there is care in the community elderly relatives are often cared for by their families, especially the women. From a Marxist perspective the elderly are certainly a burden for capitalist society because they cannot contribute economically and are therefore of little interest to capitalism. Feminists would also point out that the 'care' provided for the elderly, whether in the family home or in care homes, is usually provided by women as part of the ideology of familism. Part of the ideology of the family is the belief that women are or should be the main carer of family members. In some minority communities like those from an Asian heritage, it is thought of as normal to provide care for elderly parents and part of a grown-up child's responsibilities.

Changes in the make-up of the population have meant a reordering of the status structures of families. In the past older people were valued for their wisdom and the contributions they had made to family life during their lifetime. Indeed, in many societies today, like China, the elderly have high status and are treated with respect. However, in modern industrial society the elderly are often stereotyped as causing a financial burden, being worthless and not having a contribution to make. In families they are sometimes viewed negatively by their grown-up children, who do not have the time or inclination to look after their parents when they grow old.

However, older relatives can also make a positive contribution to families by looking after children for example. Another consequence of increasing life expectancy is that children are more likely to know and have familial relationships with their grandparents and great-grandparents. Grandparents can provide advice and guidance for the younger generation, and perhaps replace or support parents who may be busy working full time. Hence the functions and roles played in the family may change as a result of having more older relatives. It is not unusual to see grandparents collecting young children from school or looking after them in the school holidays while parents are at work. Finch and Mason have found in their study of families in Manchester that people relied quite heavily upon their extended kin for guidance, help, and financial and emotional support. Functionalists would argue that family structures need to reflect the needs of society as a whole and therefore an ageing population would need to be accommodated within such structures.

With declining death rates some marriages that would have previously ended in death now end in divorce. Hence, there are more reconstituted or blended families with associated stepchildren and parents. Serial monogamy is now a feature of modern family life. However, national statistics also show that a large number of the elderly, especially women, live alone and can become isolated from their kin and society.

This section shows appropriate use of sociological perspectives and research, making material used relevant to the question. There is also some evidence of evaluation through the discussion of positive and negative consequences. The answer generally shows sociological knowledge and understanding of the area. Concepts are applied well to the question — 20 marks. To gain the further 4 marks available, the answer would need to make evaluation points linked more explicitly to the question.

(e) The idea that boundaries between age groups and generations are becoming blurred is an illustration of the postmodernist view of society as outlined in Item 2B. The idea that a life course is a rigid and unchanging description of one's progress through life is challenged by postmodernist ideas. Generally, concepts such as age are viewed by sociologists as socially constructed, and postmodernists focus on the fluidity and changeability of such concepts over time. The rise of modernity created the allocation of roles in society to particular age groups and that is when chronological age became important so that people would know what expectations society had of them at particular stages of their life course. In other words, age became a key feature of an individual's identity during the industrial period. Postmodern society has reversed this and chronological age is much less important in determining who we are. Age-specific experience is in decline and is no longer associated with particular activities, roles or expectations. Some of these points can be illustrated in the behaviour which takes place within the family and how that behaviour has effects on the family. There are increasing numbers of teenage parents in some Western societies, age groups previously considered to be children are becoming parents themselves. Children are increasingly exposed to the 'adult' world. Children's clothes mimic adults and especially for teenage girls their dress is overtly sexualised and 'grown-up'.

> There is a good sociological understanding expressed in this paragraph. It shows a sophisticated appreciation of the consequences of the 'blurring' of age boundaries. The candidate shows that the meaning of Item 2B is understood.

Item 2B refers to adults behaving in a childlike way and vice versa. An example of this is that the leisure preferences of adults and children show a blurring of the boundaries between age groups, particularly in the family. Children are often exposed to adult TV programmes and many watch adult 'soaps', which often contain story lines about sex and adult relationships which would have been thought of as unsuitable for children in the past. Furthermore, various sorts of electronic media in the home are accessed by adults and children. Increasingly sophisticated games, play stations, wikis such as MySpace and Facebook and blogs are features of entertainment in the home for adults and children. There are also more sinister uses of these media by paedophiles who use the internet to gain access to children for adult purposes such as sex. These developments raise the contradictions of what it means to be a child or an adult. Parents want to protect their children but find that there is no clear-cut boundary between when childhood ends and adulthood begins since many children are experiencing elements of an adult world at an early age.

> This is wide ranging and well focused. Up-to-date examples are discussed and the meaning of the Item has been clearly understood.

Postman has suggested that childhood as a distinct period of time is in fact disappearing. Likewise some adults like to behave in a childlike way, dressing in younger fashions to maintain their 'young' appearance or taking exercise to keep them looking young. However, Featherstone and Hepworth also suggest that there is the development of a new industry to control the ageing process, not just fashion and make-up but also plastic surgery and HRT to keep us young. There is a whole industry that could be called 'the cult of the young'.

However, other perspectives such as feminism and interactionism would argue that what constitutes an age group such as childhood is determined by powerful adults and in fact children have little control over their lives. There is still significant age patriarchy in society whereby adults have control over children's lives.

The impact upon the family of these changing boundaries may be significant but there are also areas which are clearly designated as adult — the world of work — and others such as school which are designated for children. So to conclude we could say that some areas like leisure, attitudes and behaviour are becoming blurred in terms of adult–child experience and others are not.

✐ **Overall, this answer shows evidence of skills. There is good use of examples and research and an understanding of the postmodernist approach. The answer remains focused on the question and there is an evaluative tone throughout. This candidate is awarded 22 out 24 marks.**

Overall mark: 54/60

uestion 6

Power, control and the ideology of the family

Item 2A

According to Foucault, the family is a place of control and discipline as well as punishment. One of the main features of the family is 'surveillance or supervision of the body' as a system of individual control not unlike that of a prison, hospital or school whereby individuals are watched to ensure they follow 'procedures'. Family life involves increased supervision of members of the family by the family itself and this supervision is usually, but not always, created and controlled by adults. Bedtimes for children, mealtimes, places for eating, which rooms can be entered, times for watching television/playing on the computer, playtime, bath times — these are all examples of 'surveillance' or supervision. Adults are also controlled by social attitudes and an 'ideology of domesticity' in which family practices act to reinforce what are considered to be appropriate roles of family members. We also use 'self-surveillance' or 'self-policing' to underpin and reinforce how we should behave in our individual roles in the family as mothers, fathers, children, siblings.

Item 2B

Marxist sociologists have presented the family as a means of ideological control in a capitalist society. Through the process of socialisation children learn the norms and values of a capitalist society. The cultural beliefs of individualism, hard work, success and possession of material goods are firmly imprinted on us during our life course. There is also an ideology of familism that accepts gendered roles in the family, women as wives, mothers and domestic labourers, and men as the breadwinners. This perception of the 'natural' roles of men and women is of benefit to capitalism as women provide unpaid domestic labour and produce and reproduce the current and next generation of workers for capitalism. Women can also be drawn into the workforce when necessary as a reserve army of labour.

(a) **Give an example of a type of 'surveillance' or supervision of adults or children within the family other than those mentioned in Item 2A.** (2 marks)

(b) **Identify *two* ways in which our experience of family life may differ from the ideology of domesticity mentioned in Item 2A.** (4 marks)

(c) **Suggest *three* differences between the roles of adults and those of children in the family.** (6 marks)

(d) Examine some of the reasons for changes in the roles and relationships within the family over the past 50 years. (24 marks)

(e) Using material from Item 2B and elsewhere, assess the view that the family is part of the ideological state apparatus. (24 marks)

■ ■ ■

Task This question is for you to try yourself. You should treat it like an examination question and write the answer in 75 minutes. Plan the two 24-mark questions by making a mind map or some other kind of plan to identify the key areas to include.

For question (a), make sure your answer shows that you understand what the term 'surveillance' or 'supervision' means in the context of the family.

For question (b), ensure that you provide two clear ways in which the experience of family for some people differs from the rather stark description given by Foucault.

For question (c), ensure that you write three separate differences between adults' and children's roles. You might want to think about power, responsibilities, structure of the day, domestic labour, leisure activities, television/internet/computer use.

For question (d), you need to look closely at the changes that have taken place in the parts played in the family over the years since the 1950s. The key word is 'examine'. It means you need to discuss in detail some of the reasons why roles and relationships between husband/wife, parents/children have changed and connect these changes to what has happened in society more generally, which might have had an impact on family life — for instance, children staying on at school for longer, most women now going out to work, changes in the law to create more equality. It is always worthwhile to point out the problems associated with talking about 'the' family. You could also reflect on whether some roles have changed more than others.

For question (e), read Item 2B carefully as there is information in it that will help you understand the role of the family in relation to ideology. Make sure that you elaborate on and explain in more detail some of the points from the Item. You will gain a higher mark if you do this throughout the essay and show how you can integrate the points into your answer. Focus on the notion of the family being part of the ideological state apparatus and link the content of your answer to appropriate perspectives on the family — Marxism, feminism, functionalism and postmodernism could all be included.

Further reading

Books

Abercrombie, N., Warde, A. et al. (2000) *Contemporary British Society* (3rd edn), Polity Press.

Chester, R. (1985) 'The Rise of the Neo-conventional Family', *New Society*, 9 May, pp. 185–88.

Duncan, S. (2006) 'What's the problem with teenage parents?', *Sociology Review*, Vol. 16, No. 1, pp. 2–5.

Edgell, S. (1980) *Middle Class Couples: A Study of Segregation, Domination and Inequality in Marriage*, Allen and Unwin.

Garrod, J. (2005) 'Changes in household structure', *Sociology Review*, Vol. 15, No. 1, pp. 25–27.

Garrod, J. (2006) 'Child Support Agency', *Sociology Review*, Vol. 16, No. 1, pp. 26–27.

Hantrais, L. (2006) 'Changing family life in Europe', *Sociology Review*, Vol. 16, No. 1, pp. 28–31.

Jenks, C. (1996) *Childhood*, Routledge.

Kidd, W. (1999) 'Family diversity in an uncertain future', *Sociology Review*, Vol. 9, No. 1, pp. 11–14.

Laslett, P. (1965) *The World We Have Lost*, Methuen.

Macionis, J. and Plummer, K. (2005) *Sociology: A Global Introduction* (3rd edn), Prentice Hall.

Mintel Housework Survey (1994).

Oakley, A. (1972) *Sex, Gender and Society*, Temple Smith.

Oakley, A. (1974) *Housewife*, Allen Lane.

Oakley, A. (1974) *The Sociology of Housework*, Martin Robertson.

Oakley, A. (2005) *The Ann Oakley Reader: Gender, Women and Social Science*, Policy Press.

O'Donnell, M. (1997) *Introduction to Sociology* (4th edn), Nelson.

Parker, A. and Lyle, S. (2005) 'Chavs and metrosexuals: new men, masculinities and popular culture', *Sociology Review*, Vol. 15, No. 1, pp. 2–5.

Pritchard, D. (2005) 'What is the value of domestic labour?', *Sociology Review*, Vol. 15, No. 1, pp. 11–14.

Roseneil, S. and Budgeon, S. (2006) 'Beyond "the family": personal life and social change', *Sociology Review*, Vol. 16, No. 1, pp. 14–16.

Swale, J. (2006) 'Meet the "Neets": media accounts of the underclass debate', *Sociology Review*, Vol. 15, No. 3, pp. 22–25.

Williams, J. (2005) 'Childcare and gender', *Sociology Review*, Vol. 15, No. 2, p. 34.

Williams, J. (2007) 'Marriage and partnerships', *Sociology Review*, Vol. 17, No. 2, p. 34.

Willmott, P. (1988) 'Urban kinship past and present', *Social Studies Review*, Vol. 4, No. 2, pp. 44–46.

Websites

www.atss.org.uk

www.guardian.co.uk

www.national-statistics.org.uk